H.M.S
and ot.
1940 -   J

The Wartime Diary
of a Dental Officer

by

Surg. Lieut. Cdr. (D)
J.R.S. White, RNVR

With Compliments

J.R. Stuart White

Fractal Press

First Published in Great Britain in 1995 by
Fractal Press, Leeds.

ISBN 1 870735 05 6

British Library Cataloguing in Publication Data.
A catalogue record of this book is available from the British Library

Printed by Antony Rowe Ltd.- Bumper's Farm, Chippenham. SN14 6QA

Frontispiece
Surgeon Lieutenant Commander
J.R.S. White, B.Ch.D. RNVR

TABLE OF CONTENTS

TABLE OF FIGURES

Photographs from the author's album.

Foreword

I wish to apologise for any omissions or mistakes, such as wrongly spelt names etc. After all, it happened a long time ago and memory does not improve with age.

I would especially like to thank my nephew John S. White for his encouragement, patience, persuasion and perseverance together with his computer skills in helping to produce this account of my time in the Royal Navy. Without his help there is no doubt that the work would never have been started let alone finished.

J.R.S.W. Oct. 1994

Introduction

I was born in Dunedin, in the South Island of New Zealand on the **1st of January 1905**, both my parents being descendants of Scottish immigrants. In 1907 we came to England as my father was an engineer and wanted to learn something of the Motor Industry which was then in its infancy.

After several moves around the country, during which time my brother George was born we settled in the Leeds area where I attended the usual Primary and Elementary schools until the Great War began and then I was sent to Ackworth Boarding School till it was over and my father had returned from France. I completed my schooling at the Leeds Central High School from which I Matriculated in 1923.

By this time it had been established that I should take up Dentistry, for as my father said:

"You will not make your fortune but you will make a comfortable living."

And so it was that in the September of that year I enrolled as a Dental Student at the University of Leeds School of Dentistry. My father had insisted that I take the Degree Course i.e. Bachelor of Dental Surgery - B.Ch.D. rather than the more usual Licentiate of Dental Surgery - L.D.S. I found later that I was only the fifth to attempt the degree and that my immediate predecessor had been an Ackworthian during my time.

Naturally the degree course entailed a higher performance all the way through the five years and also included extra subjects such as Medicine and Surgery and attendance at the various Outpatients where I was usually delegated to giving anaesthetics, which came in useful in later years. In the Final Year the *viva voce* examinations on the hospital wards were the most difficult for a dental student because while the Medical Students spent a lot of time "Walking the Wards", the Dentals had to work a full rota in the Dental Hospital itself, which was run in conjunction with the Dental School - even during the University vacations.

Fortunately for me while taking my turn among the Medics during a *viva* the Sister on the ward tipped me off that the large swelling on the tummy of the 15 year old girl that I was examining was due to Lymphatic Leukaemia - and so I scraped through.

Following a brief spell of locums and a hospital appointment I opened a practice in my home village at the instigation of our local doctor who said he was tired of taking people's teeth out!

To help keep me busy during my early days I took over a branch practice in a mining village near home and also looked after a practice in Bramley for a dentist who had gone abroad for a few years. During the '30s the country ran into a depression and I ultimately gave up the mining village practice when patients' weekly payments dropped from five shillings to half-a-crown to sixpence a week, taking my chair and instruments to furnish a second surgery at my home practice.

Figure 1

The author with his wife Mary, their son David and
sister-in-law Pat Sandy.

During this period I married and by 1938 had a two year old son and with war looking imminent I decided that a career in the forces would provide a more steady income.

Figure 2

1941
Lieut. Home Guard J.Stuart White (Sen)
Surg. Lieut. J.R.S. White,
L/cp. G. Stuart White, Corps Military Police
David S. White.

1939-1941

Like father, like son, as the saying goes.

In 1914, when Father, an engineer and explosives expert, at the age of 37, went to join up the Recruiting Sergeant took one look at him and said, "This is a young man's war. Go home Granddad, we'll send for you if we need you." In March 1915 he was called up and joined the A.S.C. (Army Service Corps) as a private. He spent the whole of the war just behind the front line repairing tanks, armoured cars and motor cycles, finishing up as a Workshops Officer in charge of a large repair depôt.

In 1939, war being imminent, I decided to join the R.N.V.R. (Royal Naval Volunteer Reserve) as a friend, Roger Batley of Austhorpe and incidentally a Director of Greenwood & Batley the armament firm, was a member and used to go to sea for 14 days training every year. The Admiralty wrote back and said that at 34 I was too old for the R.N.V.R. but they were thinking of making a Supplementary List and would put my name on it. In the same year my brother George, 6 years younger than I, answered a call for motor cycle despatch riders and found himself a Corporal with the Military Police attached to the 49th Div.

On **March 1st 1940** I received my calling up papers and was instructed to proceed to Portsmouth and report to HMS *Victory,* the Royal Naval Barracks on 15th March.

I caught the 0750 train to King's Cross (it snowed all the way) then the 1240 from Waterloo arriving at Portsmouth at 2.30p.m. Having made my way to the Barracks I found they were full up and I was to take up temporary accommodation at the Central Hotel, just up the road. Bed and breakfast 7/6d, but to take my main meals in the Wardroom.

The first time I walked through the gates of the Royal Naval Barracks at Portsmouth I had little idea how I would be spending the next six years of my life.

The first fortnight was spent partly doing dentistry for the rush of recruits that was going through and partly lectures on administration, general conduct as an officer, together with drill on the parade ground, marching, forming fours and learning how and when to salute.

A retired Surg. Captain (D) was in charge of the Dental Dept. He looked the archetypal Naval character with a well-seasoned hook nose, his four gold rings and all the "scrambled egg" on his cap brim.

His second in command was Surg. Cdr. Brevitor R.N. who at least did some dentistry - as he examined in-coming and out-going drafts with a portable inspection lamp as the recruits filed past. Both the Surg. Capt. and the Commander had been brought back from retirement and I don't think I ever saw one of them in a white coat.

Hours of duty were 0845-1200 then 1315-1600. Once a week one was "Duty Boy" and on call for 24 hours during which time you had to remain within the precincts of the Wardroom. Any ship in the harbour was entitled to send a "paincase" to the Barracks at any time if the Medical Officer thought the case urgent.

There were anything from half a dozen to twenty Surgeon Lieutenants at any one time. Some stayed only a few days before getting an appointment, others stayed months. There were insufficient surgeries so one was apt to find oneself in a different surgery with a different attendant.

In the early days of the war they were all Sick Berth Reservists, St. John's men, largely from the cotton mills of Lancashire. Later they were H.O. (Hostilities Only) recruits who were made Dental Attendants only because they were unsuitable for anything else. Those in my experience ranged from a journalist on the Manchester Guardian to a St. Helens glass blower who wrote as though he had dipped a poker in the ink well.

There were six or more surgeries which we took turns to use and there was much work. The accent being on figures, figures, figures and if you did not keep up to the required number you were in trouble. We had one Surg. Lieut. in our group who was very much "agin" what he called regimentation. He was a Guy's Hospital graduate and had developed a system for treating septic wounds known as a Bunyan's Bag which enveloped the injured limb and through which a hypochlorite solution such as EUSOL (Edinburgh University Solution) was pumped. He used to take time off to lecture Medical Schools and hospitals on his system. This did not go down at all well with those in authority and after several warnings about his short-comings of which he took no notice his services were dispensed with and we saw him no more.

Occasionally a patient would be encountered who refused treatment. After everybody from the S.B.A. upwards had tried to make him change his mind - and failed - he was asked to sign the following form:

> I hereby refuse the Dental Treatment prescribed for me and understand that all claims to Pension and Gratuities be forfeited should I subsequently be invalided through causes attributable to my Dental condition.

In barracks there were usually a few awkward cases who refused treatment for one reason or another but they mostly came round in the end.

I spent most of my time exploring the Dockyard, with *Victory*, Old Portsmouth, and Southsea, the latter with the idea of Mary and David coming down for a holiday. I also took the opportunity of looking up my R.N.V.R. friend, Roger Batley who I found encamped on a cliff top on the Isle of Wight, as he put it "looking out for non-existent invasion craft" and longing to get to sea. Later, I invited him to the Wardroom for a meal and that was the last time I was to see him as he was shortly after made a Lieut. Cdr. and appointed as a gunnery Officer to *Hood*. And unfortunately he was not one of the three survivors of that ship after the *Bismarck* action. On **1st April** I was told I could "live in" and was allocated a cabin which I shared with another dental officer. My first morning in Barracks was a bit alarming as about 0600 a Wren appeared in the cabin and made off with my shoes, socks and trousers without saying a word. I lay in bed wondering what was going on but in half an hour she reappeared with a cup of tea, my shoes cleaned, my socks folded ready to put on and my trousers pressed. Still not a word. Talk about the Silent Service!

On **April 3rd** I booked rooms with a Mrs. Gill of the Norfolk Hotel on the front at Southsea, (shades of things to come) and on the 5th April I went home for week-end leave, while on my return I was warned by the Commander that I might be moving to Hayling Island.

Meals in the wardroom took place in what appeared to me to be an enormous hall with long tables from end to end and huge paintings of Naval engagements around the walls. Residents in the Royal Naval Barracks were expected to "dine in" whenever possible, especially on Guest night and had to take it in turns to be Mr. President and Mr. Vice. My turn to be Mr. Vice came on April 17th. The President and Mr. Vice sat opposite each other in the centre of the long table and after the meal the white gloved mess stewards placed three decanters in front of each of them a along with a box of broken ship's biscuit and a box of snuff. At a signal the steward on each side would remove the stoppers from the decanters. Then the President would help himself to either No.1 port, No.2 port or Bristol Cream and the ship's biscuit or the snuff if he felt like them and then pass the decanters etc., to his left and so round the table. Meanwhile Mr. Vice was doing the same at his side. When the port had circulated the President would say:

"Mr. Vice - The King."

And Mr. Vice would reply

"Gentlemen - The King!"

All seated of course - Traditionally. After a reasonable period the President might circulate the port again after which the stoppers were replaced in the decanters and the meal was over.

In the ante-room drinks were signed for on the chit system and paid for on your monthly mess bill, - and if the Mess Committee thought your bills were too high too often you were in trouble. It amused me at the formal dinners to see a Mess Steward armed with a note pad and pen walking behind the diners and noting whether they had No. 1 port, No. 2 or Bristol Cream. It all went on your mess bill.

One evening I had been on duty over at the Dental Dept. and so only had time for a quick sherry before dinner and I only had one port after my meal followed by the usual bit of ship's biscuit and a pinch of snuff. But when I got up to leave the table I felt quite dizzy. However, it soon passed off. I thought this was a bit odd so a week later I tried it again and the same thing happened so I told one of our doctors about it and he asked if I took snuff after the meal. When I said yes he replied "Well that's it - you don't smoke and snuff is largely nicotine so it will have that effect on you." You live and learn.

A fortnight later it was my turn to be President so I had the privilege of saying:

"Mr. Vice - The King."

Early in April brother George and the 49th Div. had arrived in Southampton and were awaiting embarkation for France so I went through to Southampton by train and we had a meal and a night out on the town. Here I encountered shove ha'penny for the first time though I later found it in the Mess of every ship.

In return I invited him to the Wardroom for afternoon tea. It had just been served when the Chief Steward came up and politely said:

"Sir, the Commander requests that you take your guest to one of the private guest rooms."

I replied that he was my brother and that he was on his way to France.

"Yes Sir," said the Steward "but the Commander requests that you entertain him in a private guest room."

So off we went to a little room up some stairs and there we had our afternoon tea in comfort and in private. No more was heard of my *"faux pas"* and it certainly did not worry us.

On the **9th May** Mary and David came down for 14 days and were duly installed in the Norfolk Hotel on the front at Southsea and only separated from the sea by some colourful gardens which included a yachting pond - and a tethered barrage balloon. One day we were walking through the gardens and passing the balloon which was lying on the grass "off duty" I asked David, who was only three at the time, if he wouldn't like one? He replied "No thank-you - I would rather have one of those little ones up there" pointing to one some 1,000ft or so high over the harbour. While they were down we went over to the Isle of Wight one day and also over the ferry to Hayling Island with its fine sandy beach several times.

While they were still in Southsea I got my move to Hayling Island so I bought a bicycle in Pompey for £2-12-6d and started to work there on **May 20th**, returning at the end of each days work to Barracks until Mary and David went home when I moved into the Mess on Hayling. It turned out to be one of several small training establishments on the Island and we lived in what had been a Civil Service Rest Home pre-war, now surrounded by chalets, one of which was my surgery. My boss was Surg. Lt. Cdr. Price whose house and surgery was just across the road. After about 14 days I was told to look after one of the other camps on the opposite side of the island as well which was useful as it had a tennis court and of course there was splendid bathing.

It was a very small mess of about sixteen and one morning I came down to breakfast to find the place empty apart from the elderly 2½ ringer brought back from retirement, together with the Padré and the doctor. No-one knew or would say where the others were.

It was two days before we found where everyone had been - Dunkirk. And after they eventually returned it was at least 24 hours before they reappeared in the mess - having been making up lost sleep. They had been helping to man the small boats that were used to evacuate the army from the beaches.

June 20th. I got a message from home to say that brother George was in Queen Alexandra's Hospital, Portsmouth, so after work I went along to see him. It turned out that he had had a head-on crash with another Dispatch Rider while escorting a convoy to Cherbourg, Dunkirk having been cut off. He looked a very sorry sight not having had a proper sleep or shave for some days and having a few breakages but not too serious luckily. He was surprised and pleased to see me and I went along every day to see how he was getting on. After a few days rest and good clean-up he brightened up considerably. I took him some fruit such as rasps and strawberries and by the end of a couple of weeks he was able to walk with me in the hospital grounds - but on crutches.

Unfortunately on **1st July** I got a sudden move to R.M.R.D., the Royal Marine Reserve Depot at Lympstone Barracks, near Exeter so I had to leave him but luckily he was well on the way to recovery by then. I missed a rail connection so had a meal at the "White Hart" in Salisbury and slept in the station waiting room until the milk train arrived at 0530. I had to change again at Exeter to the little train that ran down to Exmouth, leaving it about half way at Exton station from where a couple of young marines returning from leave kindly helped to carry my case a mile or so to the camp.

Arriving there I made my way to the Officer's Mess, deposited my case, had a quick wash and brush up and then went back to the Gate to report to the C.O.'s office. The C.O. was Lieut. Col. "Dolly"Dewhurst well known in the Royal Marines for a large moustache which stuck out three inches each side of his face as you stood behind him. He welcomed me to the Royal Marines, then putting one arm round my shoulder said:

"Come out and listen to my band."

And so we stood on the balcony outside his office while he took the salute as the band played for "Colours".

I soon found that the Royal Marines were a large happy family and at no time was this more noticeable than after Sunday's Church Parade when the Officer's wives and families, who mostly lived in Exmouth came into the Mess after church for refreshments. Everybody seemed to know everybody else so you would hear someone say:

"Oh, my dear, how nice to see you. I haven't seen you since Gib. or Malta" or some such place.

The Passing Out Parade of the King's Squad was also an occasion for a party as many of the parents of the young Marines would be in attendance to see them demonstrating their drill on the Parade Ground with march, counter march and rifle drill to the music of the R.M. band before the eyes of their admiring parents.

At Lympstone I found that I was sharing a surgery with Gordon Minshull who had qualified at Leeds in 1937. He had recently married and they had been able to rent some rooms in the nearby village of Lympstone so my wife and youngster were able to stay with them when they came for a holiday during the summer.

Just down the road was an attractive and popular pub and if you happened to be around about 5 o-clock in the afternoon you would find the village road-sweeper, who having left his brush and shovel and wheel-barrow outside on the pavement would ask for:

"A pint of rough please Missus."

He would take a large swig, put down his pot saying in a rich Devonshire brogue:

"Aargh! Now put a gin in it."

This was his daily routine, and a drop of gin just made the vinegary rough cider acceptable.

I had taken my trusty bicycle with me to Lympstone and used it to explore the neighbourhood and not too distant "Watering Holes." One of them was the Bridge Inn at nearby Topsham, kept by an elderly widow and her cross-eyed son and it had the extra advantage of having a full-sized bagatelle table, which was more of a challenge than the more usual bar-billiards and no one had ever beaten the crossed-son! Closing time at the Bridge was 10p.m. but if one made ones way up the hill to the very popular George & Dragon you could carry on till 10.30 .

One misty autumnal night I was making my way up the hill when I heard what sounded like a railway train approaching over the fields. I quickly realised it was the wrong place and the wrong time and guessing rightly that it was a low-flying plane I threw myself into the ditch as it roared over. Then came a tremendous rushing noise and almost simultaneously fires started all over the fields, on the road and in the hedges and I knew at once they were incendiary bombs as luckily we had had a lecture and demonstration on them recently in the camp. I continued my way up the hill, kicking a few down into the ditch and stamping out a few small fires - noticing at the time that the cows in the neighbouring field were sniffing at them curiously. Fortunately they were the early type of incendiary as the later ones exploded at the end of their performance. Needless to say I did not visit the George & Dragon that night.

I quickly discovered that Devon is all hills and not really suitable for cycling so when I saw a three-wheel Morgan Runabout advertised I quickly invested. It was a very early model with a JAP motorcycle engine of 8hp and better than pedalling. Having owned a Morgan previously I soon had it restored to order giving me something to do in my spare time. I kept the Morgan about a year till I came across a little J2 8hp M.G. for sale, the fabric covered one with a boat shaped tail. This had more "home-comforts" like a three-speed box instead of the Morgan's two and it had a hood of sorts. I found a large empty store round the back of the Sick Bay which made a perfect garage where I was able to overhaul the M.G. without fear of interruption and no one, especially the P.M.O. (Principal Medical Officer) ever knew.

In that winter of 1941, very unusually for South Devon we had very heavy snow, about three feet of it all over the camp. The Dental and Medical staff turned out and made huge snowballs which were propelled down the hill from the Mess towards the river. About the same time we had a large intake of Hostilities Only recruits from Newfoundland. They were the despair of the Instructors who said that they might be good sailors but when on the Parade Ground they all appeared to have two left feet. And the doctors found them equally stolid. When it came to inoculations there were so many of them that the docs decided to move their tackle outside and the men lined up and moved past the doctors receiving their jabs on the way. After a while one doctor began to recognise the arm in front of him. Rather worried he asked the patient how many jabs he had had. He got no answer, so asked the next one in the queue who said "Six Sir". The man was bundled in the Sick Bay forthwith.

On one side the camp was bordered by the estuary of the River Exe and on the other the ground rose up to Woodbury Common, a large area of moorland behind Budleigh Salterton and Exmouth and which was used by the Royal Marines for manoeuvres. There were roads across it here and there, and one night returning across it, when I got to the edge of the Common and could look down on the camp and nearby village I could see small fires all over the place. I stopped and watched for a while but as there was no more action I carried on back to the Camp which I found had been straddled by a stick of bombs but fortunately none actual fell in the camp itself. The only casualties were a cow in a neighbouring orchard and unfortunately the roofs of several nearby thatched cottages. The one patient in the Sick Bay heard the bombs coming and dived under his bed. Next day Lord Haw-Haw claimed the Luftwaffe had bombed the important harbour installations of Exmouth which in reality is a small typical South Devon fishing harbour only containing three or four fishing boats at the time. It turned out that we were on a Nazi flight path to and from Bristol and any bombs not already dropped were unloaded in our area.

Due to the large influx of work Surg. Cdr. George Baker R.N., our boss, arranged for a few more dental officers to be sent and so as to accommodate everybody he had a large marquee erected outside the Sick Bay containing three more dental units. There was still snow on the ground and so some oil heaters were provided. We were glad when the rush subsided and we were able to get back inside again.

In July I obtained an appointment to H.M.S. *Norfolk* to take effect from **29th August**. Cdr. Baker told me that pre-war he had been her dental officer, his surgery at that time being what in wartime was the Admiral's sea cabin on the Bridge.

When the time came for me to leave Lympstone I managed to sell the M.G. to a fellow dental officer and went home by train via Bristol. It was dark by the time we approached the city which was in the midst of a raid just then so the train stopped outside the town for an hour till it was considered safe to continue through the city.

The *Norfolk* Period

After a good leave I took myself up to South Shields where the *Norfolk* lay having been undergoing a refit after the *Bismarck* action, the *Norfolk* and *Suffolk* being the first ships to sight the German battleship coming through Denmark Straits, between Iceland and Greenland. *Norfolk* had received two hits and a fair bit of damage had been done.

Norfolk was what was known as a County Class Cruiser. Other members of the class being the *Kent*, *London*, *Cumberland*, *Suffolk*, *Devonshire* and several more. *Norfolk* was built by Fairfield's Shipyard on the Clyde in 1928 and was of 19,000 tons, with a length of 633 feet and a beam of 66 feet.

There were two boiler rooms, the boilers being oil-fired. Her main engines were turbines delivering 89,000hp and eight turbines drove four propellers giving her a nominal speed of 32 knots, which could be exceeded in times of urgency.

Her main armament consisted of four turrets each containing two eight inch guns, four dual purpose (i.e. high and low angle) four inch guns, along with two sets of multiple Pom-poms and numerous Oerlikons. She carried a crew of forty officers and 600 ratings. More in times of war.

The ship was in dry dock when I arrived surrounded by an indescribable amount of apparent chaos. There were wires and pipes of every description between ship and shore, water, fuel, electricity, telephone and compressed air, and hundreds of dockyard workmen swarming over the ship endeavouring to finish the work before returning to sea. I reported to the officer of the Watch and was then introduced to the Commander who advised me to go back home and I would be recalled when she was more shipshape, so after a quick look round I headed off home again. When I returned a week later it was a very different story, the ship was in the water and most of the workmen had gone. The dockyard gave a party and dance for Officers and crew before we actually left and I was able to have my father on board for a look round which pleased him immensely having been a ship's engineer himself for a while in New Zealand.

I found I had been allocated a cabin in what was known as the Office Flat, so-called because of the number of ship's offices there. It was on the Port side of the ship, towards the Quarter deck between a small chapel and Senior Engineer's Cabin. My surgery had been the Master at Arms cabin and was on the opposite or Starboard side, just about under the forrard 4" guns. Fortunately he didn't bear me any ill will for having been turned out.

The ship stayed a further week or so on the Tyne which I spent getting to know my way round her, checking my dental stores and putting in requests for items which I thought should have been included. My Sick Berth Attendant, (S.B.A.), Jock Smith, was a Glaswegian and had been working in the Sick Bay up to then as I was her first wartime Dental Officer. He was a very useful chap as he knew everybody, including the naval storekeepers, the shipwrights and chippies and plumbers, and so we soon had everything organised for an efficient and relatively comfortable surgery, such as an electric fire for the Arctic and a fan for when it got warmer.

Jock was also quite capable of providing (unofficially) a "chamfer up" or polish which many of the sailors wanted before going on leave. Jock would say:

"Aye lad - report here at 0800 tomorrow."

And when they arrived they were handed a tin of polish and a cloth and told to polish the corticine deck of the Surgery. At other times the would-be patient's efforts to obtain an appointment for "Beauty treatment" meant passing his tot over to Jock. The daily tot of rum (suitably diluted for ratings) was an acknowledged source of currency on board (quite unofficially of course) and a rating would do almost anything for another's tot. Officers had their own bar in the Wardroom and did not receive a rum ration.

After leaving Middle Dock we went upstream a short way to Hebburn to re-ammunition, then it was away down stream again and out to sea making our way up the coast to Scapa Flow, the big naval anchorage in the Orkneys. Once at sea we soon found jobs that needed to be done as the ship started to roll about in the seaway and things fell over. I made some racks in the chippie's shop for my medicament bottles and my air and water syringes. We also had to tie up items like the overhead dental light which was on a long arm and the same applied to the electric motor which worked my dental drill via a long cord.

The anchorage at Scapa Flow is very large and there were ships of all shapes and sizes coming and going all the time including the *Duke of York*,

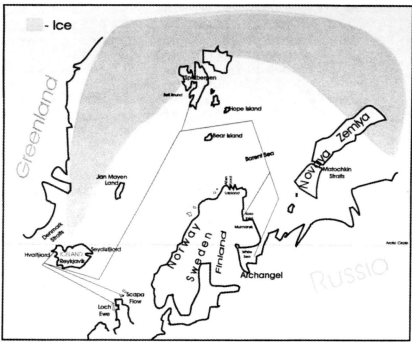

Figure 3

North Atlantic Patrol Routes

Renown, *Repulse*, and *Ark Royal* and a number of herring drifters, crewed by fishermen from Fraserburgh and Peterhead and other Scottish fishing ports. They acted as transport between ship and shore for men, stores and mail, which was distributed from an elderly ship called the *Dunluce Castle* which also housed a dental department with workshop, under the command of Surg. Cdr. Buchanan. The Flow was surrounded by islands such as Hoy, Flotta, and Mainland with the capital Kirkwall. The Admiral commanding Orkney and Shetland (known as A.C.O.S.) had a residence on Hoy and there was a small settlement with a pier at Lyness surrounded by Nissen huts for the army. One hut was a canteen which the sailors could use and another served as a cinema and concert hall for ENSA shows. Flotta was very small and boasted a nine hole golf course and a Presbyterian tea hut, presided over by a couple of Scottish ladies where after a walk round the island we would go for a tea of eggs and buttered scones for 1/6d. Dotted round the islands were isolated A.A. and barrage balloon sites, otherwise there was nothing but heather and a few cows trying to find a bit of grass.

On the island called "Mainland" is the capital Kirkwall which has a fine cathedral but it was too far away for us to visit as we were always at two hours notice for steam.

While at Scapa, "working-up" was the order of the day so the crew knew their duties automatically in an emergency. The ship put to sea regularly for gunnery exercise - sometimes they would fire at a target towed by a fast launch. Sometimes it would be a drogue towed by a plane. In both cases there were near accidents and it was pointed out that they were not supposed to destroy the target as when that happened the operation had to be cancelled. One pilot was said to remark over the radio: "I am pulling this damned target - not pushing it!"

By this time I had collected some denture work which I had taken over to the *Dunluce Castle* which in the ordinary way of things would be returned to

Figure 4

H.M.S. *Norfolk*

Figure 5

"Huge waves were streaming past."

me as soon as completed but on **16th October** I heard that we were moving out - destination unknown - so I dashed over to the lab. to find that it had not even been started so my patients would be short of their dentures until we returned. (Incidentally, if the ship moved to another anchorage such as Iceland the work would ultimately follow, though sometimes it could be as much as three months before it caught up with the unfortunate sailor.)

Almost as soon as we sailed buzzes (Navy for rumour) began to circulate - we were going to Iceland, Russia, Norway, somewhere north anyway. It quickly got colder and colder and the sea more rough, however, I had got my sea legs by now and it did not worry me even when the sauce bottle fell over on the Wardroom table.

On the **19th October** my diary reported a blue sea and sky but so cold your hair stood on end and huge waves were streaming past. I went into my winter woollies but in spite of the rough seas and motion of the ship I managed to do about ten fillings, plus a few extractions and gum treatments every day.

On **October 22nd**, we saw snow covered mountains in the distance - no it was neither Iceland or Russia but the island of Jan Mayen, an isolated spot belonging to Norway and about 600 miles west out in the North Atlantic.

That evening after dinner I got out my accordion, which I had carried with me everywhere so far in the war and gave a short recital followed by a sing-song in the wardroom. It was unexpectedly well received and we carried on until the ship began to roll very heavily, chairs were being thrown all over the place and it was difficult to stand up. Finally we all ended up in a heap with me and the accordion on top.

By **October 25th** the air temperature was 24°F and the sea 32°F. We were driving into half a gale, waves were breaking over the foc'sle, and A and B turrets. The deck was covered with snow and everything up there was frozen over. Clocks were put on one hour, which meant we were now travelling East.

Having got my sea-legs I discovered much to my surprise, not to mention that of my fellow officers, that I could continue working even in comparatively rough weather, as chair, patient and operator all moved together when the ship rolled. Though the wardroom would not believe this. They were of the opinion that I waited till the right tooth came past and then grabbed it!

Two days later clocks were put on another hour and we turned S.S.E. towards the White Sea and Archangel. At this point the Commander informed us that we were now East of Suez - which caused some amusement as the temperature was very un-Suez like. As we got further south the temperature rose, 4° and Oerlikon gun crews snowballed each other and it was noticeably warmer on deck.

During the hours of darkness, which was most of the time there were frequent displays of the Northern Lights, looking like giant searchlights as they moved around the sky, sometimes in beautiful pastel shades, moving around and changing shape all the time.

On **October 30th** there was land on each side all day, white cliffs topped by black fir trees as far as the eye could see. Every so far was a stone lighthouse and at intervals in between a wooden look-out tower with a couple of Russians armed with rifles on top. Coming to an island in the river with the picturesque name of Mudjugski we dropped anchor to await a pilot and watched large slabs of coffee-coloured ice, together with hundreds and hundreds of tree trunks floating down stream on the tide.

While awaiting the pilot the Commander took some of us out in one of the ship's motor boats to photograph the ship in the ice. A party of Russians were seen on the bank so we went over and threw them some chocolate. They motioned us to come ashore but we dare not as the sentries up in the lookout had us covered with their rifles. The pilot seemed a decent chap and had quite a sense of humour. While awaiting permission to proceed up river a submarine popped up just ahead of us. Mr. Keminski, as his name was, surveyed it for some time and then said it was one of theirs. One night we put on the film the Great Dictator with Charlie Chaplin as Hitler together with Herr Garbage and the rest of them. Keminski was most amused and roared with laughter at their antics.

On **1st November** we at last moved up river to tie up to a wooden jetty some way from Archangel but only the Admiral and his Staff, the Paymaster Cdr. and the Canteen Manager were allowed ashore there. The rest of us were allowed ashore where we were but it was a poor place, just a collection of wooden huts by the river with a small boy soldier armed with a rifle on every corner. The dockyard workers appeared to be all women, and old women at that. We tried to exchange chocolate and cigarettes for Russian badges but nearly always one of the young soldiers would come up and interrupt the swap and we heard tales of Russians disappearing to Siberia for infringing their laws against fraternisation. Anyone would have thought we were enemies instead of supposedly allies.

Later in the day a very elegant 75ft fast launch came alongside bringing back the Admiral, his staff, Paymaster Cdr. and Canteen Manager plus a patient for me. He turned out to be a young R.N.V.R. Officer needing urgent treatment. He had been on a train returning to his home up North from an appointment in S. Africa when he was whipped off and sent up to Scapa to join a ship for Archangel. He had not much more than the uniform he was wearing at the time, hardly suitable for Russia so had to scrounge warmer attire when he arrived. Otherwise he was quite happy and got on all right with the natives. The Paymaster had returned with a supply of vodka for entertaining visitors but when they arrived they scorned it, preferring our whisky.

Having given my patient the necessary treatment I had a look round the yacht while he had a meal on board. The yacht looked very smart and would not have looked out of place on the Solent in Cowes Week. I entered through the deckhouse and immediately noticed the green fitted carpet on the deck, which extended into the neighbouring wardroom. The bridge instruments and steering wheel were all in bright chrome, and the sides of the deckhouse and wardroom were panelled in bird's eye walnut. The wardroom easy chairs were covered in green moquette and there was even a baby grand piano, also in walnut. Altogether not the sort of furnishings you would expect in a Soviet ship. I went down into the engine room where there were two 800hp diesels made in Moscow, a bit rough and noisy. The ship had been built in Murmansk. The crew appeared to be part men and part women. Nobody spoke a word or asked what I was doing there.

November 2nd Sunday. Steam was ordered for 1530 on six boilers which was good news as we were all anxious to get away from this dreary place. After church on board we had a sherry party in the Wardroom to celebrate awards that had been made to the Chief Engineer and other officers for their efforts during the chase of the *Bismarck*. After lunch we were under weigh for an hour or so crashing through the ice but eventually had to stop and wait for an ice breaker as it was too thick for our thin plates.

On **November 5th** the ice breaker arrived and we slowly followed it, almost at walking pace pushing aside huge lumps of dirty ice and logs and in the teeth of a northerly gale so that we hardly seemed to move. Eventually we emerged from the White Sea and the river leading from it and were back to the old routine of Dawn Action Stations.

November 6th. It snowed nearly all day and neighbouring ships were white over. We were escorting a small convoy one of which was lagging behind so far that only its smoke could be seen on the horizon. Signals were sent repeatedly without effect so ultimately we turned back to chase it up. When we got near there was not a soul to be seen but after blowing our sirens and flashing searchlights at it for a while a man appeared on deck, ran forward and disappeared below. Shortly afterwards clouds of black smoke emerged from the funnel and it began to catch up. Obviously he had put another shovel of coal on.

November 7th. I got up at 0700 for Dawn Action Stations, hung about for an hour, had a cuppa and returned to my cabin. It never did really get light till around midday when there was a dull red glow and the sun just rose its own diameter over the horizon and then popped down again.

November 8th. Had to alter course at 0530 as we ran into thick ice, and again it did not get light all day. In the evening Rear-Admiral Wake-Walker gave a talk on his experiences at Dunkirk where he had been in charge of the small boats bringing troops off the beaches. During the day there was a gale warning and it got very rough, the ship bumping and rolling about erratically. Quite impossible to work. Finally retired to bed and tied myself in. Waves had been breaking right over the foc'sle and once I saw the quarterdeck dip right under.

November 13th. Back at Scapa and very glad to be in sheltered waters. A very large mail of letters and parcels arrived, also my denture work from *Dunluce Castle* so I shall be busy for a while. In the evening as usually happened when back in harbour, there was a Guest Night. Most people, particularly watch keepers did not drink at sea - hence the parties on arrival back in harbour. The Captain being invited, I was asked to bring along my accordion for community singing. He enjoyed it very much and complimented me on my repertoire. The Dental Stores had sent me a very nice green chair mat but first I had to get the Chippies to level the deck as the whole chair sloped outboard, tending to slide people off. They packed it up on the low side with a large slice of wood - which improved matters, so I was able to put down my nice new mat and it all looked very smart.

November 18th. Panic stations today - we have been told we are going to sea and not returning to this anchorage. Terrific excitement, everybody frantically writing letters and packing Xmas parcels. In the Wardroom we were up till 0200 censoring letters and they made me play the squeezebox while they did the work - which I didn't mind. Next day we got a lot of new people on board for passage - 180 men and fifteen Officers, making the Wardroom very crowded and smoky. Up on deck as we moved north it was quite clear and it was possible to see well down the West Coast of Scotland and the Outer Isles.

November 20th. Blowing up rough again as usual. Went to Action Stations for an unknown ship that turned out to be the *Sheffield*. A wave drove right through my scuttle and splashed right across the cabin so I hastily tightened the screws more which appeared to stop it. It got more and more rough and in the evening my bath "got up and shook me". It was impossible to stand up in the cabin, everything was falling over so I got into bed and tied myself in again. Next morning it was said to have been Gale Force 12+, and there were three or four inches of water on the mess decks forrard due to seas breaking over the ventilators and waves could plainly be heard crashing on the deck overhead.

November 24th. Had two false alarms today, both ships that had lost their convoys due to the weather and one was even heading in the wrong direction.

We arrived at Hvalfjord, Iceland after dark passing Reykjavik on the way which was all lit up like peacetime, quite a picture.

At the entrance to the fjord was a boom and a guard ship and once through that we entered the fjord proper. There were steep cliffs 1,000ft high or so and beyond the head of the fjord one could see lots of snow-covered mountains, the highest being Snaefell. It looked an interesting place and we looked forward to getting ashore and scrambling up the steep fjord sides. We soon got rid of our passengers to other ships thankfully as they took up much room.

In an anchorage the Senior Dental Officer present would allocate so many ships to each dental officer. So that almost as soon as one entered harbour a signal would arrive requesting dental appointments for so many officers and so many men.

Due to changes in weather, sailing orders etc., one could never rely on appointments from other ships turning up and so one would arrange to see ones own ship's company who were simply reappointed if in fact the others arrived.

Merchant Navy patients were also eligible for treatment and their skippers were always welcome as they usually put a briefcase down by the door with a nod and wink as though to say "That's for you!" It was usually a bottle of whisky, sometimes Aussie, which tasted like turps.

November 26th. Next day, after work, Paymaster Lieut. Giles and I got ashore in a snowstorm which continued as we scrambled up the bed of a frozen stream to the cliff top where it stopped just long enough to give us a good view of the fjord and the ships down below, after which we scrambled down and had a drink in a naval canteen before returning to the ship for a welcome hot bath. That night we were introduced to one of Iceland's tricks as at 1130 (or 2330hrs) "Clear Lower deck" was piped and EVERYBODY had to turn out, whether in bunks or hammocks in order to hoist a motor boat back on board as a fierce gale was getting up. This proved to be a frequent occurrence in Iceland and it was easy to get marooned ashore or to visit another ship and be unable to get back to your own. Similarly it would prevent patients arriving from other ships from time to time.

Not long after we arrived in Iceland two 8" American cruisers, the *Wichita* and *Tuscaloosa* plus a storeship arrived. The Yanks quickly erected their own canteen ashore and the first building that went up housed the Coca-Cola plant, so Rum and Coca-Cola became the in-thing to keep out the cold.

We came to know them quite well as we were in company with them whether in harbour or at sea all the rest of the time we were in Iceland. The only trouble with them was that the *Norfolk* was between their canteen ashore and their ships, so they would frequently call on us on their way back from their canteen just as we were about to go into dinner, so somebody had to stay behind in the ante-room to entertain them. Usually they wanted whisky, not gin and one evening one of our officers got so fed up with their constant requests for whisky (which was in short supply) that he gave one a full tumbler of Drambuie. The Yank downed it in one as usual, blinked his eyes and said: "Gee - that was sure smooth"!

November 30th Sunday. I did a little work in the forenoon and as it was a nice sunny day Giles and I decided to go for a walk ashore. We got changed and were sitting waiting in the boat when we were brought back on board for a gale warning.

December 1st. Obviously getting near Christmas as I censored 75 registered letters and twenty parcels. In the evening it was brilliant moonlight and the Northern Lights were all over the sky looking like white bands of luminous cotton wool, moving about and changing shape all the time.

December 2nd. Began what was to become our normal routine for some time, known as White Patrol. Five days out and two in harbour (looking for another *Bismarck*) in Denmark Straits. We sighted some pack ice between Iceland and Greenland. It was quite different from the Russian variety, large lumps of white milky ice floating in blue crystal clear water and as the ship went further up the Straits one could see the ice actually freezing forming a pattern like the Giant's Causeway, and known as Pancake Ice.

The surgery was over one of the boiler rooms and so it was always reasonably warm and though we had an electric fire it was never needed except in the Far North. However, when it was very cold outside the steam from the steriliser would condense on the outer wall i.e. the ship's side and freeze. Then when it melted we were in trouble as there was nowhere for it to run away and every drop had to be mopped up.

December 6th. Saw in the distance what the Commander said were the snow-covered mountains of Greenland - 90 miles away with pack ice all the way between us and the land and on which there were some Little Auks and some seals. At midday the sun was about 1° above the horizon to Starboard and the moon about the same height to Port. That day, very unusually I was handed a signal by one of the messenger boys, it was on a pink form and read: "Most Immediate - to all concerned at Home and Abroad. Commence hostilities against Japan repeat Japan at once. Timed 2100hrs."

This of course was a most unexpected shock to everyone and caused much excitement. News bulletins were coming over the air every hour and everyone was wondering how it would affect the war.

December 10th. Heard the bad news of the sinking of the Battleships *Prince of Wales* and *Repulse*.

December 11th. Next day we began another White Patrol much the same as the last until on our way back to Hvalfjord. My BIG DAY. Woken at 0300 by terrific banging and crashing and so guessed we were in the ice. Pulled on some clothes and my fur hat and dashed on deck. It was snowing, there was a brilliant moon and we were surrounded as far as the eye could see by a sea of white ice - except for a long black line down which the ship was attempting to go astern. I soon discovered the reason for the regular bumping sounds as the ship was against the ice on the port side, and the outer propeller on that side, which was about under my cabin was hitting the ice, (which looked about 6ft. thick) with every turn and it appeared to me that we would soon have a smashed propeller so I suggested to the Depth Charge sentry who was on watch in his little shelter on the stern that we inform the Bridge. He said he daren't so I said I dare and proceeded to ring the Compass platform using the sentry's phone. I got through straight away and suggested that the ship's stern be directed 5° to Starboard to get us away from the ice. There was a deathly hush at the other end as we wondered how long the prop. would last. Suddenly I caught sight of a figure approaching along the quarter deck which I recognised at once - it was the Commander and I thought to myself - now I'm in for it. But he looked at me and said:

"Oh, its you Toothie - we wondered who was giving executive orders from the Quarter Deck!"

After which I became quite famous and ever after he would introduce me to people as the only Toothwright to give an executive order on a warship. It later appeared that the Officer of the Watch at the time had only recently been married and his thoughts were probably far away instead of looking where we were going.

Next day, skirting the high cliffs of Iceland we encountered a small ship supposed to be going to the same place as us but in the wrong direction. Back in harbour there was such a big mail that I was up till 0200 reading it.

24th December. In the morning I saw some patients from the cruiser *Berwick*, seven officers and four ratings. No D.O. apparently on the *Berwick* - not as big as us.

XMAS EVE was celebrated by sing-songs in the Wardroom and for the Midshipmen in the Gunroom.

XMAS DAY. Started with a good Christmas Service in the Office flat after which the officers did Rounds with the youngest sailor dressed as the Captain and the youngest Royal Marine in the Bandmaster's uniform. We had a nondescript band - I played a euphonium - and we visited every mess in the ship having "sippers" (Unofficially) from time to time. At the Chief Petty Officer's mess I was handed a large parcel which turned out to be three pieces of wood three feet long - a hint to get started on the model of the ship that I had been talking of making.

I had been invited as the only guest to the Warrant Officer's Mess for my Christmas lunch of roast turkey and Xmas pudding, after which we listened to the King's Speech which came through loud and clear and the "Acting Captain" - the youngest sailor - proceeded to pass out - too many sippers!

We had our own Christmas Dinner at 8.00pm in the Wardroom, Giles and I sharing a half bottle of champagne (cost 3/9d) after which we had some community singing and wardroom games retiring to my bunk at 1.00am after a very, very good day.

December 26th. Did some work in the morning, a rating from *Berwick* had four front teeth smashed which I removed under Evipan anaesthetic - administered by a doctor.

Next day went ashore and having climbed up the cliff in heavy snow climbed even further till one could see over the tops almost to Reykjavik. There was a good two feet up there and we had great fun sliding down again. Back in the boat returning to the ship at 4.30pm we found we were going to sea at 6.30pm.

28th December. Had to miss church as there were numerous pain cases due to the Christmas festivities and I spent the next few days getting as many patients dentally fit as possible before closing the books for the year end.

31st December. Back in harbour. For dinner the cooks had concocted an "ersatz" or pusser's haggis. It was not at all bad especially with all the normal accompaniments. The evening was pretty dull till 1145 when the Scots element woke up and then we continued with singing and wardroom games until two o-clock in the morning and at 0400 I was woken by two of our Scots, Lieut. Kennedy and my steward Jock still "first-footing".

1942

January 1st 1942. Spent the morning stock-taking and closing my store account and totalling my Annual return which has to be signed by our Captain before being forwarded to the Admiralty. I received a signal from the depôt ship *Hecla* appointing me to survey their store account together with the Dental Officer from *Renown* so I shall have to arrange for mine to be done as well. It is usually quite a social occasion involving lunch etc. Being my birthday I treated all the lads to a drink - at a cost of 6/10d. The P.M.O. would not let us have champagne - said he was saving it for another *Bismarck*.

January 2nd. Today I began my model of the ship 1/16" = 1ft. making it 3ft 2½" in length. Later went over to *Hecla* to do their survey. Simpkins, D.O. of *Renown* was there also so I persuaded them to sign mine as we are going to sea tomorrow. On board *Hecla* I found Padré Williams who was at Exton with me. (I wonder if he was on board when she was torpedoed off Gibraltar when we were covering the Second Front later in the year?)

January 5th. At sea close to the west coast of Iceland. High rocky cliffs and running into the usual rough weather. In my spare time I started work on the hull of my model under the guidance of the Chief Shipwright Lewenden.

January 10th. Returned to harbour, received mail and some denture work. Found *Kent* in so went over to see a fellow Dental Officer, Ken Adam who also was with me at Exton and who bought my M.G. We hear they are to take over our patrol. Good!

January 12th. We went round to Reykjavik to pick up some stores and signals before going South. Reykjavik all lit up as usual like peacetime. Blowing a gale but fortunately it was off the land. Left at 6.30am in a very severe gale with terrific seas, much damage on the foc'sle so we had to turn back and take shelter. Anchored off Reykjavik. Later it turned out that a heavy sea had bashed in the side of "A" turret and the next lifted off one half of its roof, hurled it up as high as the bridge and then it fell on "B" turret. (The half roof was said to weigh two tons). The people on the bridge had a lucky escape but one seaman was killed and several injured in the turret.

January 14th. 0900 on our way again as the gale had moderated. Meanwhile the shipwrights had been making a temporary roof for the turret from timber. Still extremely rough and I was again unable to work as the motion of the ship was too violent. The engines were said to be turning over for a speed of fifteen knots and we were only doing five. At one point the ship registered a 45° roll - I thought it was never coming up again. The forrard mess decks were again flooded, seas were coming down the ventilator and fan shafts and the forrard messes had to be evacuated.

January 16th. We have now had three bad nights in a row and it is still too rough to work.

January 17th. Woke up this morning to find we were thankfully in the anchorage at Scapa.

January 19th. Guest night in the Wardroom to say Farewell to our Skipper, Capt. Phillips who is leaving. He made a speech and particularly thanked R.N.V.R. types for their part in running the ship. After dinner we had some Scottish dancing, with me on the accordion, followed by the usual wardroom games, in the course of which the P.M.O. knocked out our Capt. of Marines - Captain Ruffer needing a few stitches!

January 20th. Went ashore at Lyness to an ENSA concert, very good and a nice change. Later, during the evening I was called to the surgery to see a rating who had fallen and smashed a front tooth which I devitalised and will crown later. The new captain has arrived, Capt. Bellars R.N. and it is said that he has asked if there is a dental officer on board.

Captain's Rounds:

At 11 o-clock on a Thursday morning Captain Bellars would do his "Rounds" of the ship. He was preceded by a Royal Marine bugler who sounded off a "G" at intervals as they passed along the alley ways followed by First Lieutenant and a selection of Divisional Officers. After the warning "G" from the bugle he would inspect the various ship's messes, the Sick Bay, the Galley, the ship's offices and anywhere else that occurred to him.

When he arrived at the Galley the Paymaster Commander would be awaiting him - it being under his charge. Our Paymaster was a wily old bird and from previous experience he knew that if the Captain could just find one little thing wrong, such as a dripping tap or an unwashed mug he would be happy and move on. So our paymaster had evolved a little game. He would hide a potato in some fairly obvious corner, then when the Captain discovered it he would draw the Paymaster's attention to it and pass on, and all would be well, honour satisfied.

It is said that on one occasion when our Paymaster's thoughts were elsewhere he forgot all about the potato and the Captain searched high and low for it without success. Eventually he said:

"All right Pay. I give up, you have got me beat this time - Where have you put the perishing thing?"

My dental steward "Jock" had his own methods of keeping the Captain happy. He always made sure that I had a patient during "Rounds" even if he had to be press-ganged into the chair. The Captain would look in to the surgery and seeing I was apparently occupied with a patient he would say:

"Ah Toothy - I see you are busy so I won't trouble you," and pass on his way.

On the other hand, the Dental Surgery was one of the Captain's favourite show places whenever he was showing some visiting Brass Hat around the ship and then, of course, we welcomed him in. He was a great chap and I always got on well with him.

January 21st. Mail on board including our family 8mm Cine camera and some film.

January 22nd. Due to the recent violent gales there is a great scarcity of crockery in the ship so that some messes of twenty men only have one mug to drink out of and perhaps a jam jar or two. And there are none left in the Stores ashore as every ship is in the same position. The Captain organised a competition for the best device to make drinking glasses out of bottles, which the Chippies won. It was a wooden framework which held the bottle. A length of line was wrapped around the neck with a man each side pulling alternately. Then when the bottle neck was hot it was whipped out of the frame and put neck down in a bucket of water, when the top of the bottle came neatly off. I finished the hull of the model today and it is ready for painting.

January 23rd. Very busy in the surgery as there are rumours of leave and everybody wants to be "on top line". Left Scapa.

January 24th. Woke up to find we were in Rosyth, anchored just above the Forth Bridge. We left Rosyth about midnight and sailed South passing through a north bound convoy in a snow storm - by Radar - without seeing any of them!

January 25th. The ship also entered the Tyne in a very heavy snowstorm and the first we knew was when we noticed that we were passing houses on the harbour side. We went up river first to de-ammunition and then returned and went into Middle Dock where we were to have repairs to the damaged turret and two new tripod masts fitted as a result of the extra weight up top from all the various radar aerials that ships were having to fit.

January 26th. Having obtained the Captain's permission to go on leave I packed my bag and left at 5.30pm by a special train that came into the docks, bound for Newcastle where I managed to snatch a sandwich and a cuppa for 6d. from a W.V.S. trolley. Then caught a very cold Leeds train where I was jolly glad to be wearing my "Glamour pants" and seaboot stockings, ultimately arriving at Leeds where I was met by father.

February 10th. I returned to the ship, extracted some teeth for the P.M.O. and fitted some immediate dentures for him, saw a few pain cases, had a look round the ship and then went home again till recalled on **17th March**. Changed to the London-Newcastle train at York which fortunately had a buffet car where I had a slice of veal and ham pie and a beer.

March 19th. I found we were going to be in the Tyne for another week so phoned home and arranged for Mary to come up for a few days. She arrived at 8.30pm and we put up at the Royal Turk's Head. Meanwhile I dealt with various pain cases and gum treatments as the surgery was in good order once more.

March 20th. Went into town in the morning, did some shopping and we bought a Cossor wireless set from Binns for my cabin, then went to the Eldin Grill where we had a huge grilled sole after which we went to the ship's dance at South Shields where Mary met the Captain and several of the ship's officers.

March 23rd. Sunday. Brought Mary down to the ship and showed her the surgery and my cabin where we were brought lunch with drinks from the bar by James our bar steward.

March 24th. A warm and sunny day. Mary returned home so I took our two Canadians, Tiny Lambert (6' 6") and O.H.M. Wright for a walk along the coast towards Whitley Bay via Cullercoats where we had afternoon tea at the Park Hotel.

March 28th. In late March, the convoy PQ13 with the brand new light cruiser *Trinidad* as escort had sailed for Murmansk. Nearing Kola Inlet the convoy was attacked by three of Germany's largest destroyers. After a fierce fight *Trinidad* managed to sink one destroyer and badly damaged another, which she attempted to finish off with a torpedo. Unfortunately it went "wild" and started to circle round finally returning and hitting the unfortunate *Trinidad* amidships and making a huge hole sixty feet by twenty feet. Fortunately the enemy withdrew and *Trinidad* was able to limp into

Kola where there was plenty of dockyard labour but no repair materials which had to be brought from England.

We sailed at 9.30pm and arrived at Scapa next day with good views of the Outer Hebrides and the snow-covered mountains of Scotland on the way.

We spent the next few days in and out of the Flow doing gunnery and other trials. In the surgery I had plenty of work with much gum treatment, usually using Chromic acid solution followed by hydrogen peroxide. Always after leave there would be an outbreak of Vincent's disease, an infection of the gums, sometimes patients had to be admitted to the Sick Bay and isolated as it was very contagious. The sailors, of course had caught it from the lassies ashore. Their drinking vessels and plates all had to be segregated and sterilised after use.

The ship had been "degaussed" against magnetic mines while in dock which were the latest of Hitler's weapons. "Degaussing" meant passing an electric current through a cable right round the ship which demagnetised the steel hull so avoiding setting off the mines.

One day a number of big ships came into the Flow including *Renown*, the *Duke Of York* and *King George V* battleships, the aircraft carrier *Victorious* and the cruisers *Liverpool*, *Kent* and *Charybdis*. A most impressive sight.

Nothing much of note during the next few days. Principal operation being painting ship. One rating fell in the drink but was rescued O.K.

April 1st. A lovely summery day. We went out in the Firth to do an 8" shoot on a battle practice target. I watched from the bridge and was nearly deafened. I tried to film the big guns as they fired but jumped so much I was quite unable to hold the camera still.

In the big ships with 12" and 14" guns it was necessary for the dental staff to dismantle the surgery equipment and pack it safely away each time there was gunnery practice but our 8" guns did not worry us a great deal though we always stopped work, mainly for the sake of the patient's nerves.

April 3rd. Good Friday. Went ashore with Lieut. Mitchell R.M. and Giles. We walked to the Officer's Club and had a tea of baked beans, tomato and Tiddey-oggy - a well known dish in the South-west, usually known as a Cornish pasty.

April 5th. A wet day so no Divisions. I fitted a crown for the boy (Catterall) who had fallen down a ladder on the last cruise and smashed a central incisor. He was amazed at the result and could hardly believe his eyes.

April 6th. Out all day with the U.S. Cruiser *Tuscaloosa* for an 8" shoot and returning to my Cabin found that the black and white cat had had kittens in one of the trays under my bunk, one of which was stillborn.

April 8th. The convoy PQ14 left Iceland for Russia on the 8th April with *Edinburgh* as escort and carrying a number of large steel plates for the repair of the *Trinidad*. They encountered thick fog, with the ice further south than expected. They were soon spotted by the enemy, several merchant ships being lost. The remainder reached Kola Inlet on the 19th April having spent many days in fog and frost.

April 9th. Two more kittens, again one stillborn, the rest OK. There are strong "buzzes" around that we are moving out soon for an unknown destination. Sounds like another convoy?

April 11th. Mother's birthday. I had sent her a little bottle of Devon violets perfume in a leather case with the ship's monogram on it. We moved out of the anchorage today and heading North as usual.

April 12th. Dawn Action Stations 0530 - horrid! Came back to my cabin to find the cat yowling and wailing. It had slept on another kitten, the best one too. Only one left - an all black. Definitely going North, we have been told it will be twilight all night.

Today developed a wheezy cough so stayed in my bunk. Visited by Doc. "Wullie" Weir and the P.M.O. who put me on Menthol inhalations every two hours. A very unpleasant night with waves smashing against my scuttle.

April 13th. Still inhaling for bronchitis though my "tubes" seem to be clearing a bit. The ship went to Action Stations today but I had to stay in bed. I heard that two ships of the convoy had been sunk and one had run itself onto the ice. We spent the night chasing a Radar echo which finally disappeared seventy miles short of Spitzbergen, our furthest north so far.

April 14th. "Hands pipe down" announced today on account of having been at Action Stations all night.

Today I stopped inhaling but was given a bottle of medicine. The cat brought its kitten out for exercise for the first time. It seems to get about all right but persists on going round in circles in an anti-clockwise direction. Today the convoy was sighted and I was allowed to get up for supper. I was shown the Snow Bunting that flew on board during a snow storm. The Snow Bunting became the ship's symbol as several more came on board from time to time, and each one seemed to bring "Action Stations" with it. Commander Litchfield had this one stuffed and put into a glass case which still exists and appears at the Annual Reunion.

April 15th. Woke with a sore throat and am inhaling again. It had been twilight and "Action Stations" again most of the night. We have been recalled to Iceland, and during the day had to suddenly take violent avoiding action - a 60° turn at 25 knots - possibly avoiding a torpedo? Also heard that we have lost some more convoy.

April 18th. Approaching Iceland we met *London* coming out and were "bombed" by a Walrus aircraft which dropped a small bag on deck containing a message "Welcome to Iceland"!

April 19th. A sunny day, glad to be back in harbour but unable to go ashore because of my cough. The kitten's eyes are now open.

April 20th. Had to do a little work in the morning on pain cases and gum infection which is still rife. But I still have a pain in my chest and retired to my bunk in the afternoon. Meanwhile hands are busy painting ship.

April 22nd. Still painting ship. In the evening we dined the Captain after which I got the accordion out and we had community singing. Six foot six inch "Tiny" Lambert, one of our Canadians was pushed through the hatch of the Bar after James decided it was closing time! - around 0200!

April 24th. Sailed around midday and relieved *Belfast* on "White Patrol". Visibility good about six miles.

April 26th. Nice sunny day though windy. Managed a short walk on deck and then visited "Slops" as the clothing shop on board is called and bought three shirts at 3/3d, two ties at 1/9d, three pairs of socks and six collars, total 19/2d.

April 28th. On this date the convoy QP11 which included the *Edinburgh*, with Admiral Bonham-Carter aboard and which was carrying five tons of Russian gold (payment for Lease-lend) sailed from the Kola Inlet with a destroyer escort.

On the **30th April** she was attacked by three large German destroyers and struck by two torpedoes, one hit her amidships and blew up a boiler room, the second blew off the stern, rudder and two outer propellers. She could still move slowly ahead but due to having no rudder went round in circles. In spite of this, when one of the enemy destroyers crossed her bow she managed to hit it with her two forrard guns and it finally sank. An attempt was made to tow the *Edinburgh* back to Murmansk with a tug, but the enemy returned and managed to hit her with a further torpedo and she had to be abandoned on the 2nd May. Survivors, including the Admiral, were taken on board the destroyers.

Dawn Action Stations 0200 - 0300. Returned to my cabin to find a wave had burst through my scuttle and soaked my bed. Only the mattress escaped.

Today we went through a tremendous flock of Little Auks, or Dip-chicks. Black with a white pinnie. They cannot fly but skim the surface and then dive.

April 30th. Saw some large trawlers in the distance, also a Hudson aircraft of Coastal Command. Later, while having tea I heard and felt an explosion. The Hudson had unaccountably dived into the sea and its depth charges had blown up. The crew had climbed out onto a wing but when the depth charges went off they were caught in the blast and although they were brought aboard and efforts at resuscitation made there was no hope for the poor chaps who were later buried at sea.

Going back into Hvalfjord we watched Puffins on the rocks, their red beaks showing up very well.

May 1st. Went ashore with Giles, Wright and our American Lieut. Russell and walked to the Yank canteen along a shocking road, mostly dirt, although it was the only road round the island. It presumably gets carried away every year during the winter. We met several of their officers including a dental officer and a doctor. They were from the U.S. ship *Melville*, a store and destroyer depôt ship to which we were invited to lunch later in the week. We got a lift back to our ship in their boat.

May 4th. Had lunch aboard the *Melville* which started with lettuce salad, then soup followed by stew and boiled rice, cookies and sponge cake with icing and chocolate sauce and coffee. There was unlimited fruit, lettuce and celery. How the other half live! I was shown round the ship which had a very smart dental surgery with Ritter Unit and X-ray. The meals were served cafeteria system and you collected what you wanted on a partitioned Stainless steel tray. The crew's cabins were all central heated with their own air conditioning, while the kitchen was fitted with dish washers.

May 5th. Next day I had the opportunity to go into Reykjavik - in the back of an army truck. The road was bad all the way and extremely dusty and we arrived white with dust. It took half an hour to do the first seven miles and the whole journey of thirty-five miles took 1½ hours. However, the scenery was good although dangerous as we crossed a number of narrow bridges, some of them without side rails. We did not think much of the town with its wooden houses and corrugated iron roofs, not a tree in sight apart from a few shrubs and dwarf Rowans in peoples' gardens. There was not much of interest in the shops either but I managed to buy some tweed at nineteen Kroner per metre which seemed cheap. I finally returned to the ship on an Icelandic fishing boat, and stood on deck all the way on account of the stink of fish down below.

May 6th. I parcelled up the tweed and sent it home as we are sailing this evening. Note, Reykjavik looks much more attractive from the sea. It was light all night so there were no Dawn Action Stations and the sun was still well up at 10.30pm.

May 10th. A fine warm day. There are lots of little brown speckled land birds flying along with us and alighting on the ship from time to time for a rest. The Commander said they were Wheatears migrating to Iceland for the summer. We have been ordered to return to Iceland and re-fuel. Wonder what's in the wind?

May 12th. We left Hvalfjord at 0800 and are moving East, past Reykjavik and between Iceland and the Vestermann Islands which look like a sailor's death-trap, being huge jagged rocks and mountains sticking straight up out of the sea with a tiny village at the foot of one. Later we clearly saw the great glacier, Vatna Jokull as it swept down to the sea.

May 13th. We had picked up our convoy during the night and are accompanied by *Kent* through intermittent snow storms with occasional Arctic Skuas flying alongside us. The sun was still up at midnight and one could plainly see the Jerry shadower keeping his eye on the convoy but staying well out of range.

May 15th. Still being shadowed and went to Action Stations from 10.45 to 1800 and were dive bombed at intervals for two hours. Both *Kent* and *Liverpool* receiving near misses. We heard that several planes had gone away smoking and also the bad news that *Trinidad* had finally been sunk. On this day the repaired *Trinidad* had sailed from Kola carrying Admiral Bonham-Carter and other *Edinburgh* survivors but was again attacked by heavy enemy forces, finally sinking after a whole day of air and torpedo attacks. Survivors were brought back to Iceland by the destroyers including the Admiral who said it was his fifth sinking.

We had a peaceful night though everyone slept in their clothes, being still at Action Stations. Our air cover arrived a bit late - at 1700 or 5.00pm. after which we turned for home accompanied by *Kent*.

May 18th. Back in Hvalfjord again, Adam, the Dental Officer of the *Kent* came over and I took out an inlay matrix for him, he having lost a gold filling apparently. After which he stayed for lunch.

May 20th. I fitted Adam's gold inlay which he had cast on his own ship.

May 22nd. We sailed from Iceland with the *Kent* and several others. It was a fine sunny day without any incident but fog came down during the evening.

May 23rd. Still foggy. The ship went to Action Stations but it turned out to be a false alarm - a Polish destroyer in the fog which had forgotten the code word. At 0100 we oiled a destroyer, it being light all night.

May 24th. Empire Day. Still foggy. Went to Action Stations again over the same Polish ship.

May 25th. We have a convoy of sixty ships and "Wearie Willie" as we call our Jerry shadower has been circling us all day. Sometimes a ship gets fed up with him and fires off a few rounds. Usually without success but it makes him weave about a bit. A flight of Jerry bombers arrived at 11.45pm and another lot at 0120 and the Cam-Hurricane plane was sent up to break up the flight and do what damage he could. We were told he brought down one Jerry and damaged another. The Cam-Hurricane was a special plane mounted on a catapult on the bow of a merchant ship. When its operation was complete, or when it was about to run out of fuel it had to come down in the sea - preferably as near one of our ships as possible. The convoy got off very well, one small ship had a steam pipe fractured and had to be towed back to Iceland. The remainder carried on and at 0300 had to run the gauntlet of the U-boat fleet lying in wait between North Cape and Bear Island.

Some time later there was a paragraph in the paper to say that Pilot Officer Alistair Hay had been awarded the D.F.C. for his part in dispersing the attack. This was the first time that the Cam Hurricane had been employed. There was only one to each convoy and when you had shot him off that was that. They bravely filled the gap until the Light Aircraft Carriers converted from American banana boats began to arrive.

May 26th. There was another "flap" at 0300 and the ship successfully dodged two torpedoes. A number of depth charges were heard during the night as we manoeuvred in mist and ice. The German ships *Admiral Scheer* and the *Lutzow* are said to be at sea but they did not turn up. On the way back the *Kent* left us for Iceland while we were to return to Scapa after picking up a homeward bound convoy.

May 28th. Back in Scapa I went aboard our flagship *Duke of York* to obtain some stores as I was running out of filling materials. Surg. Capt. Williams, the fleet Dental Surgeon invited me to tea with him.

May 30th. We had a Guest Night for Doc. "Wullie" Weir who is leaving us.

May 31st. Sunday. We had Divisions by marching past the Captain followed by church. In the evening I was invited to dinner in the Warrant Officer's Mess and took the accordion with me for a good sing-song.

June 2nd. Had two officers and four ratings over from *Liverpool* for treatment. In the evening the Warrant Officers gave a concert. I accompanied some of their items and our Bar-steward James gave an hilarious impression of a glamorous Wren.

June 4th. I made a couple of small vases in the Plumber's shop out of pom-pom shell cases. During the day we had a sub-calibre shoot in the Flow and nearly hit a small trawler!

June 5th. I went aboard U.S. Cruiser *Wichita* for lunch with our Warrant Officers. We had boiled ham with baked apple and sweet corn followed by sultana tart, cheese and biscuits and coffee. I met their "Toothie" nick-named "Jerky Joe" Clements. He came from Georgia. He also had a nice surgery with the latest Ritter Unit, a CDX X-ray and a proper operating theatre working light - but he had no scuttle so could not see out.

June 6th. Great preparations for inspection by H.M. The King who came aboard at 3.00pm. The ship's company marched past by Divisions, including me with the Sick Bay Staff. Our Chief Plumber had made a little replica of an Admiral's uniform cap in silver which His Majesty appreciated very

Figure 6

A distant view of Iceland from "A" turret.

much and I managed to get some of the action on film. In the evening I attended a ship's dance on Flotta, with Wrens, Nurses and ATS. I won a spot prize! Our Captain dined aboard the U.S. battleship *Washington* with the King that evening.

June 10th. I treated some officers and ratings from the small cruisers *Scylla* and *Phoebe*.

June 11th. In the afternoon we went to a very good ENSA concert in the cinema at Lyness and were entertained by Bobby Hind's Band and the Hot and Sweet Singers. They were very good and they were invited back on board for refreshments. In the evening we had a Guest Night for "Tiny" Lambert the Canadian Engineer Officer who is reluctantly having to return to the Royal Canadian Navy.

June 12th. One of Wichita's float planes crash landed alongside their ship, having lost a float taking off. It spun round and then capsized and was hoisted aboard. All the crew were O.K.

June 13th. The Fleet Dental Surgeon came on board and inspected the surgery and invited me to have lunch with him on board the *Duke Of York*. He wants a plan of the surgery accurate to one inch. Obviously he approved of our layout.

June 14th. Captain's rounds this morning, he had a quick look round and then inspected the model which is looking well now and causes much interest.

I went aboard the *Duke Of York* for lunch and found Adam of *Kent* there too, also *Liverpool's* dental officer. Mainly talking shop.

June 16th. Doc. Wright and I took our ciné cameras ashore on Flotta and filmed Arctic Terns which dive-bombed us continually while we filmed their nests among the pebbles on the beach. The tern's eggs were olive coloured, splodged with green. Later Doc. trod on an Eider duck on its nest in the heather which flew off with a great commotion. Its eggs were as big as a goose egg and were all green.

June 17th. We are to return to Rosyth to exchange a gun and arrived there on the 19th, 7.30pm. The Port Dental Surgeon, Surg. Cdr, Osborne came on board with one of his assistants Surg. Lieut. Cdr. Horne. They had a look round the surgery and then said I must take advantage of the opportunity and go on leave, or get my wife up for a few days - and they would deal with any emergencies or pain cases, which I thought very decent. Later I went into Dunfermline to the Dental Stores to replenish some of my stocks and then spent some time attempting to phone home without success. Finally I returned to the ship and phoned from there. Even so I did not get through till

1.00am, much to the disgust of Mary and her sister Pat for disturbing them at that hour. However, they agreed to get the train to Edinburgh where I had booked rooms at the Royal British Hotel by the station and they arrived next day.

June 21st. I took Mary and Pat down to the ship in the morning and showed them all round including the Galley, the Bakehouse and the Bridge etc. having both lunch and tea onboard in my cabin.

June 22nd. We did some shopping in the morning followed by lunch at Mackays and in the afternoon took a bus bound for North Berwick which proceeded to have a head-on crash with a small lorry on the way. Fortunately nobody was hurt apart from the lorry driver. But it was a bit of a shock all the same. North Berwick is a pleasant little seaside town and we had tea there before returning.

June 23rd. Mary and Pat returned home and we sailed at 10.30am after thanking Horne the Assistant Port Dental Officer for looking after my patients for me. Arriving back in Scapa at 10.00pm.

June 24th. The ship left Scapa at 0400 in fairly rough weather though I managed to do some work in the surgery after which I started making the tripod masts for the model out of steel knitting needles bought in Reykjavik.

June 30th. Arrived in Seydisfjord about 0900 but did not go far in unfortunately, anchoring near *London*, *Wichita* and *Tuscaloosa* who were already there. The fjord sides are very steep and mountainous with jagged tops, 1,000 - 3,000ft high covered in snow which was blowing off like a white cloud. There were a few small houses or farms at the foot of the cliffs and that was about all.

July 1st. Left Seydisfjord at 0030 in a fairly calm sea. The Yanks flew off their float planes regularly all day, spotting for ice and German subs. They have a better way of recovering the planes than we have. They drop a mat affair over the stern onto which the plane climbs and then it is hoisted aboard by a crane.

July 2nd. Much colder today, back to winter woollies. We have just passed between our out-going convoy and the homeward bound one though they are out of sight. Fuelled the American destroyer *Wainwright*, interrupted by an air-raid alarm which did not materialise. Our Walrus was flown off at 9.30pm on an anti-submarine patrol then the fog shut right down and we lost it till 0100 next morning when it returned safely. Meanwhile Admiralty had reported that air reconnaissance of Trondheim Fjord had shown that the German battleship *Tirpitz* was absent and it was assumed that she was travelling north to intercept the convoy which had already sustained several attacks from JU88s, both bombers and torpedo carrying planes, and had lost one American merchantman at the cost of two of their planes.

July 3rd. Several alarms during the day as enemy aircraft were spotted. We even fired three rounds of 8" at one who was getting too nosy, after which he flew off and disappeared. Our Walrus was flown off again at 9.30pm for an anti-sub patrol and we heard depth charges exploding in the distance. We are now North of Bear Island.

July 4th. "The Glorious Fourth" I don't think!

Some excitement was caused this morning as at 0001 all the American ships struck their ensigns in unison. However, they were not surrendering *en masse* as the rest of the convoy imagined. To everybody's relief they hoisted huge brand new ones to replace the dirty tattered and smoke-stained ones and then the penny dropped. It was their Independence Day.

However, they did not have long to celebrate as wave after wave of bombers and torpedo planes arrived and so it continued for most of the day in spite of very vigorous defence by the convoy and its escort.

Our ship is only 800 miles from the Pole, near Hope Island, which is South of Spitzbergen, and during the day we went to Action Stations at least ten times.

The Walrus was sent off again at 2000 (8.00pm) and we then got a signal - too late - not to fly it off as it had been confirmed that the *Tirpitz* had left Trondheim and was even now in Alta Fjord which is right up on the north coast of German occupied Lapland and within easy striking distance of the convoy.

Expecting this to happen the convoy was ordered to scatter and we were ordered back to Iceland. An attempt was made to get the Walrus back but probably because of the weather they did not get the message and so, at the end of their patrol they returned to the appointed area to rejoin the ship to find us gone. After hunting around for a while the Walrus located the Ack-Ack ship *Palamares* and came down alongside her. The crew were taken on board and the Walrus taken in tow.

Meanwhile we sped off, four cruisers and eight destroyers through fog and between icebergs and all the time wondering what was going on and why we were leaving the convoy, fog horn going from time to time and each ship towing a fog float astern for the benefit of following ships.

July 6th. Foggy again most of the day. We oiled two more destroyers and also met up with the Home Fleet who had been informed that the *Tirpitz* and other German big ships were out which was why the convoy had been told to scatter.

Still believing that the *Tirpitz* was rapidly approaching the convoy had scattered in all directions thus becoming easy victims of the U-boats and dive bombers. There were soon calls for help from the Russian Air Force, without avail. Some ships made north to the edge of the ice barrier in order to get as far away from the German air bases as possible. Another group made for Novaya Zemlya and the shelter of Matochkin Straits which runs between the two islands. Here they were joined later by those who had sought the safety of the ice and who had in the meanwhile painted their ships white for camouflage and so there were fourteen of them in all.

It was decided to investigate the Straits in order to ascertain if it would be possible to go through into the Kara Sea and so creep down into the White Sea. So some fuel was found for the Walrus and it flew off to investigate. Unfortunately, the Straits were completely blocked with ice so after due consideration it was decided to attempt to reach the White Sea by sneaking down the side of Novaya Zemlya and entering the White Sea unobserved. Fortunately fog came but then they ran into an ice field from which they only broke out with difficulty. And having arrived in the approaches to the White Sea they were spotted by a Blohm & Voss spy plane which called up the dive bombers and they lost two more ships before at last tying up in a Russian port on 11th July. And there they remained for over a month till a stronger convoy with aircraft protection could be organised to accompany them home.

July 7th. Back in Hvalfjord, followed by *Wichita*, *Tuscaloosa*, *Renown* and *Kent*. During the day we heard very unhappy news about the convoy which was now scattered all over the Barents Sea, North of Norway and being attacked by aircraft and submarines.

July 10th. After work some of us took a small boat over to "Puffin Island" and climbed up onto it to photograph the hundreds of funny little birds who did not seem to mind our presence at all.

July 12th. Our Paymaster Comdr. organised a picnic ashore for some of us today on the far side of the fjord. We lit a fire on the beach and had an excellent lunch of Tiddey-oggies that had been made by the cooks and were at least ten inches long overall. Very good indeed, followed by fruit. We had just settled down on the beach after lunch when a patrol of U.S. Marines appeared with fixed bayonets and arrested us in spite of our Paymaster's protests, and proceeded to march us off to a hut in their camp about a mile away. It turned out that we had lit our fire on a buried ammunition dump! Once in their camp we were bundled into a hut, and it appeared that no-one there had authority to release us and we were there all afternoon until somebody got through to someone in authority who had us released. Our Paymaster was very cross!

In the evening we had a sing-song in the Warrant Officer's Mess at which Douglas Fairbanks Jnr. who is on board the *Wichita* should have attended with others of their W.O.s but he had been recalled to London and flown there by Catalina.

July 18th. Some while back our Captain had suggested that the ship hold an Arts and Crafts Exhibition to see what sort of talent there was, he being no mean artist himself. It was held today and produced a truly remarkable range of exhibits including paintings, drawings, model ships and aeroplanes, children's toys and wool rugs and tapestries. My model was very well received though I was barred from the competition as they said I had an unfair advantage. Later the Captain took it to his cabin to show visitors.

July 19th. I went aboard *London* to see their P.M.O. who puts ships in bottles. Convoy PQ18 is assembling in the fjord, 43 ships in all. We had a walk ashore and found a snipe's nest with three babies.

July 21st. Sailed at 0930 with *London* and *Kenya*.

July 23rd. Action Stations 0330 - 0430 and went back to bed again as nothing appeared to be happening. Going South towards Scapa we could see Cape Wrath in the distance.

July 26th. While at Scapa we heard that Rear-Admiral Bonham-Carter and his Staff are coming on board for three weeks while *Sheffield* goes into dock for repairs. This means that most people will have to move cabins to make way for them. It also means that the Wardroom will be very crowded while they are with us.

July 28th. Today there was a Damage Control Exercise which meant I got no work done during the morning. The whole ship would be involved in the exercise. All lights were extinguished and power cut off. My Action Station had to get a "casualty" who had been lashed in a Neil-Robertson Stretcher, and haul him up by rope from down in the aft engine room. He was about three decks down and had to be hauled up steep ladders. It was very hot and I was wringing wet. I was always glad of my Boy Scout training on those occasions as it was my responsibility to attach the rope to the stretcher.

July 29th. Admiral Bonham-Carter hoisted his flag at 0900.

August 4th. Went ashore at Lyness to an ENSA concert. There were live marionettes, and a burlesque conjuror among other items. Afterwards some of us had tea at the Scottish tea hut. Back in the ship I posted off a parcel of tweed.

August 23rd. Went aboard *Jamaica* and had dinner with their dental officer Hall and Lacy of *Suffolk* who was also there.

August 24th. Went aboard *King George V* with a letter for the Fleet Dental Surgeon recommending my S.B.A. for promotion to "Leading Hand".

August 26th. After four weeks and four days we at last sailed for Iceland and Hvalfjord. During the day heard that The Duke of Kent had been killed in an air crash on his way up to Iceland. Doc. Donovan went into Reykjavik and brought me back some more wool for home. It is very cold for August.

August 29th. *TODAY I HAVE BEEN ONE YEAR IN THE SHIP.*

Went for a walk ashore up into the mountains. Already some snow about and lots of good waterfalls.

Lieut. Russell of the U.S. Navy who is one of our officers, and I had dinner with the Admiral. His Flag Lieut. and our Captain were also present.

September 1st. While the Jolly boat was being hoisted the sling broke and tipped its driver into the drink but he was none the worse. Today there was an opportunity to order some cloth from Akureri, which is up on the north coast and famous for its tweed. I ordered four yards of brown for the family at 16Kr or 9d a yard and two yards of green tweed for a sports jacket for myself. It is said to be stronger than Donegal tweed and lasts forever.

September 2nd. Went ashore for a long hike and picked about 3lbs of "blueberries" which I had for breakfast for three days. Climbed up to a huge waterfall which descended in a succession of cascades. We dined the Admiral in the evening after which he did some conjuring tricks for us.

Meanwhile the convoy PQ18 which had been assembling at Loch Ewe in Scotland had sailed for Archangel after a long delay (due to the demand for carriers and destroyers in the Mediterranean at that time.) The convoy had an escort of seven destroyers and five armed trawlers as far as Iceland where more destroyers, minesweepers, an Escort Carrier and an anti-aircraft ship, the *Scylla* with Rear-Admiral Burnett in command, joined them.

The cruiser force consisted of *Norfolk* with Vice Admiral Bonham-Carter, *Suffolk* and *London*, together with *Cumberland* and *Sheffield* which were taking supplies to Spitzbergen.

The convoy was in four ranks of ten ships which turned out to be very difficult to control as many were either American or foreign, for whom it was their first convoy and losses were to occur because they were not used to flag signals and did not respond quickly enough to avoid torpedo attacks.

The convoy ran into bad weather almost immediately and ships became left behind but fortunately caught up in due course. It was soon sighted by

Figure 7
Doc Weir and the author.

patrolling Blohm & Voss planes who kept watch and radioed course and numbers to the German Headquarters in Norway.

Between Bear Island and Spitzbergen U-boats were waiting and although our escorts managed to sink one, three of the convoy were torpedoed shortly after.

From then on there were continual attacks by U-boats, dive bombers and torpedo-bombers for three days and nights until the convoy turned South for the White Sea and Archangel, and on the 16th and the 17th they met the homeward bound convoy QP14 to which Admiral Burnett transferred with the *Scylla*

Due to the presence of the Escort Carrier *Avenger* together with the anti-aircraft ships PQ18 had lost ten ships out of forty, whereas PQ17 only had thirteen survivors out of the thirty-four ships that started.

N.B. The port of Archangel could not be used in the winter as the White Sea froze up and could not be used till the ice broke up in early summer, so the new port of Murmansk was developed as it remained ice free during the winter owing to receiving the tail-end of the Gulf Stream with its warming influence. The main disadvantage of Murmansk was its proximity to the German occupied border.

September 8th. Ashore for some exercise climbed the fjord side and over the next range and then up what looked like a volcano cone, mostly shale and porous rock. Great for sliding down!

September 9th. There was a party in the W.O.s Mess, it being the birthdays of Percy Quantick, the Chief Shipwright and Mr. Worrel, a Warrant Gunner. The Captain came in for a while and took part in the community singing. He said I was a human card index of songs and tunes. A good party and no after effects.

September 13th. A very rough day and none of our boats were lowered. A large party of "Brass Hats" arrived for a conference in spite of the weather among whom were said to be a number in khaki. It was also said that the sound of dogs barking could be heard from *Cumberland* which later turned out to be true as *Cumberland's* hanger had been turned into kennels for huskies!

September 14th. Sailed at 1030am, fine at first but it turned into a screaming gale. *Suffolk, Cumberland* and *Sheffield* and three destroyers were in company with us. We are taking winter supplies also a pack of huskies to a small garrison on Spitzbergen also acting as a covering force for PQ18 before picking up the returning convoy QP14 on the way back. We hear that the out-going convoy has been dive bombed and that two ships have been sunk.

September 15th. Dawn Action 0600. *Suffolk* disappeared to investigate a strange ship which turned out to be a tramp steamer. We oiled the destroyer *Bulldog* in a snowstorm otherwise it was a better day. Had another Medical Station practice involving hoisting up the heaviest stoker from the depths of a boiler room.

The returning convoy QP14 had left the White Sea this day with fifteen merchant ships, many of which were carrying survivors of the ill-fated PQ17. Initially they had an escort of two anti-aircraft ships, two destroyers, four armed trawlers and two rescue ships until joined by Admiral Burnett with the *Scylla* and attendant destroyers on the 17th. The German planes left them alone but they were continually attacked by U-boats, losing the destroyers *Leda* and *Somali* together with three merchantmen before arriving in Iceland, and then Scapa on September 26th.

September 17th. It is getting even colder and we had the surgery fire on for the first time. We have arrived at our appointed destination but there is absolutely nothing to be seen. We just have to stooge around and keep watch while the others go in and unload which is a slow process as the quay is very small and there are no facilities, everything had to be manhandled.

September 18th. Still snowing at intervals. *Cumberland* has disembarked her stores and huskies and *Sheffield* has gone in to do likewise. Our ships do not appear to have been observed by the enemy, whose camp is on the other side of the island. Meanwhile we go up and down, round and round in the same bit of sea keeping watch. Today I started to make the

Walrus aircraft for my model out of balsa wood. *Sheffield* has returned and we have turned for home.

September 21st. Sunday. Had a few pain cases today and then finished the Walrus model. It looks quite good and I shall camouflage it like ours.

Heard that QP14 had been in trouble last night with subs and that *Somali* had been torpedoed and taken in tow by *Afridi*, both Tribal Class destroyers. She was towed for four days then she broke up in a storm.

September 22nd. Roughest night for a long time and had to lash myself in again and fasten things down to stop them rolling about. Far too rough to work. We hear that *Amazon's* rudder has been damaged in the storm and she is steering with her main engines. We got in at 1800hrs.

September 23rd. A farewell sing-song for the Admiral and his staff who is transferring his flag back to *Sheffield*.

September 26th. Had a long walk ashore, to a waterfall at least 300 metres high about twelve miles away and said to be the highest in Iceland. Very rough going and we got very wet fording several rivers. Luckily a fine sunny day.

September 28th. Had a treat today. I went into Reykjavik with a party on board the destroyer *Oribi* and returned at 2100hrs arriving back at the ship at 2315. It was a grand day, sunny but cold. I bought some more wool, silk stockings and varnish for the model. Had both tea and dinner at their best hotel, "The Borg", *hors d'oeuvres*, salmon trout, steak and a whipped cream sweet. I walked all round the town and viewed its housing estates but all very monotonous and no trees except stunted Rowans in peoples' gardens. On the way back there was a good show of the Northern Lights. I had spent about 169Kr. altogether.

September 29th. Another trip to Reykjavik was arranged for today so I sent my S.B.A. Jock. It was not such a good day though as a gale blew up and they got very wet on the way back. In the evening the ship went to Anchor Watch.

September 30th. We were unexpectedly sent to sea with *Suffolk* as we hear that a suspected raider is attempting to come down through Denmark Strait. It blew a gale all day and I was quite unable to work so went up on the Bridge for a while when the sun came out and filmed waves breaking right over the foc'sle and as high as the Bridge itself.

October 1st. We are still beating up and down. Still very rough - took part of a wave through the surgery scuttle which wet things a bit and during the night the waves were still banging against my cabin.

Figure 8

H.M.S. *Kent* - a near miss.

October 2nd. It snowed really hard all day and we had two alarms - *Suffolk* shot out of a blizzard right across our bows and the other turned out to be the destroyer *Oribi*. There was half an inch of snow on deck and the temperature was 26°F. Although there was a heavy sea I managed to do some work including a gingivectomy which was a change.

October 4th Sunday. Back in Hvalfjord we had a walk as far as the volcano cone "Black Mountain". There were several feet of snow in places and we saw a herd of thirty or more Icelandic ponies being driven from one valley over to another. They were all different colours, shaggy little beasts.

October 7th. I received a parcel containing apples and pears from home - in good condition too - also some ciné film from father.

October 9th. Due to gales which suddenly swept down the fjord we were at anchor watch all day. Three officers and thirty-six ratings joined the ship for passage - I wonder where we are going now?

October 10th. *Berwick* arrived from patrol to relieve us and we left immediately, heading out into a very heavy snowstorm arriving at Scapa next day without incident.

October 13th. Went ashore with Doc. Donovan and walked to Stanger Head and saw Athey who used to be D.O. of the *Tyne*. He has his wife here and seems to be enjoying life fishing, shooting and boating. We then walked along to the Club where we had two boiled eggs each for tea. During the night we left for Greenock and had a very rough passage after getting clear of the Outer Hebrides.

October 16th. We turned into the Clyde early this morning passing Ailsa Craig (Paddy's Milestone) followed by Wee Cumbrae and Big Cumbrae and anchored up the Clyde opposite Greenock. I had leave to go with the first Liberty men but there was no Leeds train till 9.30pm so had a meal at the St. Enoch Hotel to pass the time. I had a comfortable journey as the train was warm for once and arrived in Leeds at 0330 so took myself into the Queen's Hotel where the Night Porter got me tea and a cheese sandwich, after which I dozed till 0730, washed and shaved and then rang Thorner. Pat came and fetched me and we returned via Halton where everybody was well.

October 21st. Time to return to the ship so left Leeds at 10.30pm and returned to Glasgow by York, Newcastle and Edinburgh. I took sandwiches with me and had a comfortable warm journey again.

October 22nd. Arrived at Glasgow at 0530 and caught the 0630 to Gourock but found that the ship had not yet come down the river from the shipyard so had breakfast and lunch at the Naval Club and rejoined her with some others at 3.00pm after some difficulty in getting a boat.

October 23rd. Next morning we got under way at 1100 and had a good trip down the Clyde meeting a large U.S. convoy coming in and passing several big liners full of troops obviously all ready to go somewhere. Going down the Clyde we got good views of the Cumbraes, Dunoon, Bute, Arran, the Mull of Kintyre, Northern Ireland and Islay before it got too dark.

October 25th Sunday. Back in Scapa again. In the afternoon we went for a walk on Hoy for a change along past the remains of German warships scuttled after the First World War. Now all bottom up and being slowly demolished for scrap. We had a poor tea at the Risa Tea Hut as they had no milk and little to eat.

October 27th. Out all day for gunnery exercise with *Cumberland* and *Renown* but it was very rough with poor visibility and too uncomfortable to work.

October 28th. I went over to *King George V* to see the Fleet Dental Surgeon who was very pleased to see me and gave me lunch after which we talked much shop.

October 29th. A rough day in the Flow but managed to get ashore at Lyness to an ENSA concert which consisted of eight girls and two men and was quite good.

October 31st. There are lots of "buzzes" going round the ship and it would appear that something is afoot. Doc. Donovan and I went ashore on Flotta and had a good tea at the Church of Scotland Tea Hut as usual and got back on board to hear that we are sailing at 11.00pm under sealed orders - not to be opened till after midnight!

November 1st. We are heading South and the "Buzz" is that we are off on a Big One, perhaps the biggest of the war but do not know our destination yet. Most people think it is something to do with the Second Front.

November 2nd. Dawn Action Stations at 0715. We are in company with *Cumberland* at eighteen knots. Everybody is very excited and wondering what is going on.

November 3rd. It is getting warmer and the ship is said to be about level with Spain. The temperature on my surgery thermometer read 74° until they decided to test the 4" guns just above, the shock blowing it off its hook and smashing it. I sent my S.B.A. down to Stores to draw another. After lunch I sat on deck in the sun for half an hour. There was a long gentle swell and it was very pleasant. Quite a change from our usual conditions of ice and gales.

November 4th. The ship is now on a level with the Azores. It is getting hotter all the time and everybody is doing a bit of sunbathing when off duty.

November 5th. We are patrolling between Madeira and the Azores.

November 6th. I am now working mornings only on account of the heat. We had a submarine warning at 3.00pm and heard depth charges but saw nothing. We oiled *Offa* and passed her some fresh bread from our bakery and some books and received in exchange a large number of pineapples as they had recently been into the Azores. An unexpected treat. We had several Sub. contacts during the day but nothing conclusive. Possibly shoals of fish. We hear that our troops are doing well in Africa and have 20,000 prisoners already. We oiled *Offa* and *Onslow* today. (Rumours that the *Hecla* has been torpedoed. She sank while they attempted to tow her to Gibraltar.) Tough luck - a most expensive ship - she had been up in Iceland for some time and was a sub. depôt and repair ship.

November 8th. As we had expected, our forces and the U.S. had landed last night along the North Africa Coast at Oran, Algiers and Casablanca and all going to plan it appears. We hear that the Governor of Algiers has ordered the people to do what they can to oppose the Germans. I took some film of the Walrus flying off and circling round over *Cumberland*. It landed later in a heavy swell breaking the propeller, damaging the body and one wing. Might as well throw it over the side! We were ages getting it hoisted in by the crane - in fact so long that I had time to go below for a new film. Anything could have happened.

November 9th. Today I made one propeller for my model and cast another off it, in white metal. Now I have to make two more for the other side. All our convoys have got through safely according to the Radio news though one was dogged by Subs. for five days. We hear that we are to go into Gib. for fuel.

November 10th. A very hot morning - the temperature in the surgery rose from 80°F - 86°F during the day. Although we cannot see any land yet we can smell it on the wind, like the scent of flowers. It is a dark starry night and the ship is leaving a phosphorescent wake.

November 11th. I was up this morning at 0700 not for Action Stations but to see the Straits of Gibraltar. I was surprised how narrow they are - no more than eight miles with the Moroccan coast quite clear and the Atlas Mountains rising in sharp peaks behind. We arrived in Gib. at 1000 and entered the small harbour and put in place by tugs. *Nelson* was there with two carriers and masses of destroyers. We left again at 4.00pm after fuelling. Only the Messman got ashore and he returned with oranges, grapes and bananas - first time I have had a banana for years! While we were alongside I went up on the bridge and had a good look at the Rock with the powerful Bridge binoculars. Could see the people quite well but not the famous apes.

November 12th. Last night as we went back through the Straits there was an electric storm with much lightning and the lights of Tangier were very clear. We are now going northwards and there are two large empty liners going with us, returning for more troops. The *Monarch of Bermuda* and a Polish ship, the *Batory*. The *Monarch* is exceptionally steady and does not appear to roll, certainly not as much as we do. We are keeping up about eighteen knots. It is still hot and sticky below decks but blustery up top. Lieut. Russell, our American says the *Monarch* and the *Queen of Bermuda* were built for the Bermuda crossing as people were not going because they were seasick on previous ships.

November 14th. Today we have been fourteen days at sea and as we return North it is noticeably colder with a pretty rough sea. Even the *Monarch* is shipping a sea over her bow from time to time while the *Batory* does so regularly.

November 15th. In England the church bells are being rung to celebrate the victory in Egypt, I heard them clearly on my wireless.

November 16th. The *Monarch* and *Batory* left us at 1100 while we wend our way up the West coast of Scotland through the Minches.

November 17th. Arrived back in Scapa at 1800. A nasty damp and misty day but loads of mail waiting for us.

November 20th. While we had been at sea, a lot of us, with the Captain's permission, had grown beards - or attempted to, and there were some surprising efforts from big bushy ones to small pointed ones, like mine, on the chin only. When we want to get rid of them one has to get the Captain's permission to "shave off". (While the beards were growing they were inspected to see if the result was suitable for a Naval Officer!) I kept mine on for the rest of my time in the ship and shaved off after I got home. This evening we had a Charlie Chaplin film of the Gold Rush, the old silent film to which had been added speech and music. It was good to see it again.

November 24th. Today we had a damage control exercise with no lights or power in the ship so I was unable to work between 0930 and 1030.

During the day I received a telegram from A.C.O.S. - Admiral Commanding Orkney and Shetland - advising me of the Birth of a Daughter! The wire read:

"23rd daughter arrived all well."

Which Pat had sent. There was much leg-pulling and remarks such as:

"How are the other 22?" etc.

I had the Warrant Officers up at lunch time and we all wet the baby's head.

November 25th. We had a lecture and slide show today by Seton-Gordon, the naturalist, about seals and Arctic birds. It was very good but he is a better writer than speaker. Also a letter from Pat saying that Mary woke them at 0230 on the 23rd and it was all over by 0430 when Frances Elizabeth was born weighing 8lbs. Good Show!

November 27th. I went ashore to an ENSA concert at Lyness. A very good show. Two girl accordionists, two comedians and a concert party. We brought them back on board for High Tea and then we all had a sing-song together with one of them playing my accordion. They would have a rough trip going back as the wind had got up but they had had plenty of drink by then to help them on their way.

November 28th. Sunday. We went ashore to Lyness and walked to the Church of Scotland Tea Hut. It is a very indifferent tea these days not half as good as when Miss Campbell and Mrs. MacFarlane ran it with their home made cakes, drop scones etc.

December 1st. It has snowed all day for the last two days so I have spent some time working on the model as there is an Arts and Crafts Exhibition at the end of the week.

December 2nd. Went out for a shoot but it was not much good because of the snow and too rough for me to do any work so we returned to the Flow to hear that *Suffolk* had been damaged in a storm and we were going to Iceland to take her place. In the evening we had a practice with our "Squeegee" band consisting of two accordions, six mouth organs and three mandolins. After which we were up till 0200 censoring letters.

December 3rd. I had two parcels from home today - not to be opened till Christmas! A long time to wait. We sailed at 2.30pm with *Cumberland* for Hvalfjord.

December 5th. Approaching Iceland the usual gale developed and the lights of Reykjavik looked bright and jolly from the sea as we passed.

December 7th. After dinner we had a party for Kennedy, Sid Mitchell (W.O.'s Mess President) and Bob Read our Canadian Senior Engineer. The party went on till 0400 but I didn't!

December 8th. Today we had another very successful Arts and Crafts Exhibition though not as well supported as the last one as so many "Rabbits" had been sent home as Xmas presents. ("Rabbits" - object made from materials scrounged in the ship - usually for presents).

December 9th. We are now practising every day in the "Dogs" (Dog Watches) for the concert which is due to come off at Christmas. I have been busy writing and transcribing music for our musicians for a while now.

December 13th Sunday. I did a Gingivectomy for a change this morning for Sub. Lieut. Gibson which went well. It was packed with Sulphanilamide powder and he was given three tabs of M&B693 for three days. Healing was uneventful.

December 14th. I had to get our little Cornish Blacksmith Pascoe to make me a small surgical mallet to enable me to remove an unerupted wisdom tooth for a patient, which was lying horizontally. I drew it to scale and it should have been about eight to nine inches long, with a steel head and haft. A few days later he proudly produced a most beautiful HAMMER with a steel head all right but a haft of wood about fourteen inches long (which I still have). I had to be very tactful, so I thanked him and said:

"Now Blackie - can you make me a miniature one about eight inches long with a steel handle?"

And so he did and it worked admirably and I used it for years after the war. Although the Admiralty provided me with the necessary small chisels there was no mallet with which to hit them.

December 15th. I went over to the Yank Store ship *Vulcan* and saw their double dental surgery. Naturally it was very smart and all the latest. They gave me "cawfee" cheese and biscuits, sticky chocolate cake and doughnuts for lunch.

December 16th. We heard through our Padré Ken Mathews that the R.A.F. in Iceland were short of games like draughts, chess and so on and that they had some Bass mouth organs to swap and I was all set to fly to Reykjavik in the Walrus when the wind got up and the flight was cancelled. Pity. Later the Commander said we could go in a lorry that was returning, so Doc. Donovan and I climbed into the back of this lorry and after being jolted about for two hours we arrived in Reykjavik smothered in dust and after some trouble found the R.A.F. Padré who gave us lunch and we received two beautiful bass mouth organs in exchange for two dartboards, several packs of cards and some books after which we made a quick dash to the pier and managed to get a lift back to the ship in the destroyer *Icarus* arriving at 3.00pm.

At 11.00pm the ship put to sea for a White Patrol. I had just enough time to send my Christmas cards over to Lewin in the *Blenheim* before we sailed so he could get them into their mail. We tried out the new mouth organs and they are terrific. They weigh about 2lbs each and make a grand thumping bass sound.

December 18th. No Dawn Action this morning but a scare at 0930 which turned out to be three U.S. merchantmen presumably going round to Seydisfjord to join a convoy. It got light about 1030 and the clouds above Iceland glowed for a while and then it got dark again an hour later.

December 20th Sunday. We have been among floating pack ice all day, known as brash. I did another gingivectomy today. I do these on a Sunday so I can take my time and not be disturbed.

December 21st. The wind got up during the night and I had to tie myself in. During the day the rolling was too erratic to do fillings so did a few extractions instead. There was a very colourful sunrise at 1230 and it set again at 1.30pm. All colours from electric green to thermogene pink. Later, 10.00pm I was called out to a "bleeder". It was from an Upper "8" socket and I put in three sutures after smoothing some rough bone edges, then sent him off with a Veganin.

December 22nd. Returned to harbour, peaceful after the gales outside.

December 24th. Xmas Eve. We spent all the morning rehearsing for the concert which is to take place this evening. The queue started at 7.00pm though the concert was not due to start till 8.00 o-clock. All available space in the Office Flat had been built up by the chippies with seating for about 500. All went off well, notable numbers were The Squeegee or Harmonica Band, the Warrant Officer's item, which I accompanied, Bar Steward James as Miss Greta Gangrene and The "Basookaphone", a weird and wonderful home made instrument. The Captain and all officers available attended and it was thoroughly enjoyed by all.

December 25th. Christmas Day. The day began with the usual church service followed by a fancy dress parade round the ship. We had numerous visitors from other ships in the wardroom and then had a buffet lunch. In the evening we dined the Captain and then had a sing-song till 12.30pm. Voted a very good evening with no rough stuff for once.

December 26th. A normal morning's work after which the sailors had a darts match followed by an "Uckers" Tournament which was terrific. "Uckers" is like Halma. The contestants wore fancy dress and each "thrower" of the dice had a Manager and Trainer. The dice was fully one foot square and was tossed in a barrel, being both a test of strength and endurance arousing noisy enthusiasm from the spectators.

December 27th Sunday. I slept in - not surprisingly! During the Dog-watches we had a Gala Whist Drive after which Captain Bellars made a speech thanking all those who had helped with the festivities and specially singled me out for my efforts with the Band. Was my face red!

December 28th. I went over to the *Blenheim* to have lunch with Capt. Blackman and see his workshop where he makes model ships. He was building a model of the paddle-wheel frigate *Vulture* of the early days of steam, amazing detail putting my work to shame. However, he was very

Figure 9

The Author's Model of H.M.S. *Norfolk*

kind, gave me some tips! and promised me some fine anchor chain.... mine is a bit outsize. When Capt. Blackman makes a model he does it the way they would build a real ship - laying down the keel first, then the ribs, planking the sides and even putting in the decks down below and lots of their fittings that will never be seen, rather than my method of using three solid pieces of wood glued together on the sandwich system. After leaving the Captain I had tea with Lewin, their D.O. and returned to *Norfolk* as we were having a Musical Quiz in the evening. The first we have tried and it went down very well. I had to play the clues on the Squeezebox.

December 29th. The anchor chain came over this morning from Capt. Blackman. It is beautiful, very fine and just right for the anchors which I had already cut out of brass plate. So I soon had them installed and they look great.

December 31st. Unexpectedly sent to sea on a White Patrol - on New Year's Eve! A very cold day, the temperature on deck being only 20°F at 10.30am.

In the evening we had a half-hearted Hogmanay and the Warrant Officers came up and we all sang Auld Lang Syne and sixteen bells was struck to signify the end of the Old Year and the beginning of the New.

Summary of the Year's Work

Taken by and large the navy is very "Tooth-conscious" as witnessed by the fact that when I joined the ship my Dental S.B.A. already had a long waiting list of would-be patients. Most new members of the ship's company had already been made Dentally Fit before they joined and usually only required maintenance work from time to time. There were accidents of course, mostly caused by falls on wet or icy decks or down ladders. Fractured incisors gave me the opportunity to use the (then) new acrylic material and make crowns for their smashed front teeth which were always well received, mostly believing they would need a denture.

A lot of work, particularly after shore leave was caused by sailors returning on board with gum infections (Vincent's Disease). Vincent's produced swollen and bleeding gums which took a lot of clearing up and was time-consuming. The only way of treating it at this time was with the application of a solution of Chromic acid followed by Hydrogen Peroxide several times a week, sometimes for several weeks. Severe cases were admitted to the Sick Bay to be treated with antibiotics. They were kept in isolation with their own mess traps so as not to infect others as if neglected this condition could quickly spread through a whole ship. (Occasionally I had to supply chromic acid and peroxide to S.B.A.s from other ships so they could treat their own crew members.) In some patients this condition recurred frequently and then I would perform a gingivectomy which removed the swollen pockets round roots of the teeth where the infection tended to resist treatment.

On the few occasions that general anaesthetics were required they were administered by one of the doctors, and when I required an X-ray I used their portable outfit, e.g. for a Royal Marine who sustained a broken jaw in a ship's boxing match.

Both the sailors and the officers greatly appreciated their dental treatment, which they would not have received on smaller ships, as only the larger ones like battle ships, aircraft carriers, depôt ships and the bigger cruisers carried dental officers.

Note, that when in harbour preference had to be given to patients from other ships and you treated your own ship's company while at sea.

There were several advantages in being a dental officer on board. Firstly, you were only responsible to the Captain - the one exception being at Action Stations when the D.O. came under the jurisdiction of the P.M.O. If, as sometimes happened the P.M.O. or any other officer in the ship interfered with your work or life on board in any way, which you thought uncalled for you were instructed to forward the details to your Fleet Dental Surgeon, and he, if he thought fit would pass the message on to your Captain who would suitably deal with the case.

Another advantage of being a dental officer was that you were accepted by the crew more readily than one of the ship's officers particularly if you helped in the ships entertainment in any way.

Summary of years work aboard Norfolk 1942

```
Fillings of all types . . . . . . . . . . . . . . . . . . . . . . . 1,137
Extractions . . . . . . . . . . . . . . . . . . . . . . . . . . . 450
Scalings . . . . . . . . . . . . . . . . . . . . . . . . . . . . 200
General anaesthetic . . . . . . . . . . . . . . . . . . . . . . . 8
New Dentures . . . . . . . . . . . . . . . . . . . . . . . . . 36
```
Gum treatment (Vincent's Disease) there were 152 appointments purely for gum treatment. Some cases recurred and had to be treated repeatedly.

1943

January 1st. Quite the worst birthday I have ever had. Terrible weather, three inches of snow on deck and a beam sea which keeps crashing against my cabin. Fortunately we were recalled at 4.00pm and were soon on our way back to our Anchorage - thankfully.

January 2nd. Arrived in Hvalfjord. A very cold day with much snow still on the deck.

January 3rd. Today is even colder, the morning temperature being 12°F rising to 15°F at midday. The Dental Officers of *Belfast* and *Cumberland* came on board to do my Stores Survey, and stayed for lunch. Several sailors who had been ashore got their fingers frozen through holding onto the drifter's rails, as the deck was a sheet of ice.

January 5th. A nice day though cold. I went over to the *Cumberland* to do their survey and was invited to stay for their Guest Night, being seated next to their Commander who was Mess President. A good dinner with few speeches. I returned in the drifter with our Royal Marine Band which had been giving a concert on board *Cumberland*.

January 6th. A very bright day. The sun is rising noticeably higher and lights up the distant mountains with a rosy pink glow.

January 10th. Today we had our postponed Christmas turkey and very good too.

January 13th. Eight officers from the U.S.S. *Vulcan* came over for dinner including their Dental Officer who hailed from Virginia. He and another of them fell in the drink going back to their ship.

January 14th. Today we went out for an 8" and 4" shoot with *Cumberland*, *Blenheim* and *Vulcan*. Medical parties were exercised as usual - extricating "bodies" from inaccessible places below decks and in the dark.

January 19th. Some of us went to *Cumberland* to their concert followed by supper. It was a good concert, more ambitious than ours and they also had the advantage of a hanger which not only accommodated more but gave them a bigger stage.

January 20th. We had a walk ashore up to the head of the fjord, and a shooting party under Capt. Ruffer R.M., brought back a brace of mallard. The river was well frozen over and there was plenty of ice everywhere.

January 23rd. We went out for an 8" shoot but the weather was not suitable - fog and snow and it was too rough to do any work in the surgery.

February 5th. A very rough night. Although we are in the fjord we are at one hours notice for steam, in case we have to move anchorage. A Force 10 gale is blowing and the ship is lying across the fjord with waves roaring past all night.

February 6th. Still at one hours notice, but eventually left for Scapa.

February 8th. Arrived at Scapa where I was pleased to get some long awaited denture work, which will please some of my patients.

February 10th. I went over to *King George V* to see the fleet Dental Surgeon.

February 11th. In bed all day with a bilious attack!

February 18th. We left Scapa at 0830 encountering heavy weather outside, so much so that I was unable to work.

February 20th. The ship arrived off Seydisfjord, Iceland, at 1600hrs. during a blizzard so we had to plough up and down all night awaiting better visibility for entering.

February 21st. Entered the fjord at 0930 finding *Sheffield* there, with a damaged turret, and *Cumberland* who passed us four R.A.F. officers and fifty ratings for onward passage to Russia. We all three left at 1600.

February 22nd. A Focke-Wolfe Condor was sighted, its four engines clearly visible. They are long distance planes but it fortunately left us alone and was probably on a weather patrol to Iceland.

February 23rd. Snow showers and half a gale today but I managed to do some work even managing to fit a crown. At 1800 we closed up to Action Stations for the passage of Bear Island. We should be overtaking the convoy somewhere here but did not see it due to the blizzards.

February 24th. We are still at Action Stations. I am two decks down in the Officer's bathroom flat which is down near the stern and very cold. I am wearing my thick pyjamas, seaboot stockings and a jersey under my battledress and rolled up in an old blanket. We sleep on the stretchers and manage to keep reasonably warm. I wonder what is going on as we listen to the various bumps, bangs and crashes of the attack. Now and again the Commander gives us a running commentary over the inter-com. I went up top about 0400 to see what the weather was like. It was blowing very hard and we were doing 24 knots into it. Doc. Hart and I took it in turns to go up for a breath of fresh air. The galley sent us snacks and jugs of tea from time to time which was very acceptable, and in between whiles we played cards and crib. We have now passed Bear Island and are within 60 miles of Norway's North Cape. The convoy is OK so far.

February 25th. Spent all day again closed up and expecting air and surface attacks but none materialised.

February 26th. We finally arrived at Kola Inlet Murmansk at 0500 after a quiet night and the convoy went straight on to unload. Looking out at 0730 I found we were alongside a wooden jetty in a little bay off Kola Inlet called Vaenga. There was not much to see apart from wooded slopes and a few huts on the quayside. During the morning I went ashore and had a walk round. There were plenty of Russian soldiers and sailors and dockside workers who all seemed to be old women. Some people were wearing skis and there was two feet of snow everywhere. During the day I heard that there was a Naval hospital not far away with two British doctors and a dental officer.

February 27th. Some of us were invited on board the Russian Destroyer *Baku* which was lying nearby, for lunch. We were taken over in one of our boats which was then supposed to return to the ship but the crew was invited on board by the Russian sailors and "treated" - unknown to us, with unfortunate consequences - as it turned out.

My first impression as I boarded the ship was of the appalling stink of the Heads that seemed to permeate everywhere. However, we were taken down to their Wardroom, six of us, and about eight of their number of whom the only one that could speak much English was their Commissar who had been to a British University. Every Russian ship had a Commissar among its crew. They are not seamen but government spies whose job it is to ensure that both officers and men keep to the Soviet rules. There were several glass jugs of what looked like water on the table which of course turned out to be Vodka - Archangel Vodka they said, with a slight aniseed flavour, whereas our variety seems to have no taste. The glasses luckily were small as the meal began with a Toast and continued with Toasts in between each course, and at each you had to empty your glass which was then promptly filled again. We toasted Our Glorious Navy, the Russian Glorious Navy, our Victorious Armed Forces, the Russian ditto. We toasted Winston Churchill and Marshall Stalin, and we toasted the Second Front - whenever that was going to be. This was the most important matter to them - the Commissar asked us over and over again:

"When are you going to open the Second Front?" as though we should know.

The meal otherwise was excellent and amongst other items consisted of Vladivostock Crab, Turkey of the Sea, which was a large fish from the Black Sea, and Strawberries from the Caucasus. All Very Good.

We had barely finished the meal when our Gunnery Officer, Lieut. Willis came bursting into their Wardroom saying:

"You are all under arrest, return to the ship at once!"

It turned out that our boat had become untied and was drifting down the river and had been spotted from our ship. So we had to return to the ship in ignominy but full of Vodka, to be told off by the Commander. Goodness knows what the Russians thought and I don't know what happened to our sailors.

In the evening some of the ship's company went to a cinema ashore where they were showing a film of the Victorious Russian Navy taking over the convoys from Britain when they reached the dangerous waters nearing Russia. There were naturally loud boos from the audience.

February 28th. The Dental Officer from ashore, Surg. Lieut. Kettle, and one of their doctors came on board *Norfolk* in the evening for Dinner followed by a film show which was a nice change for them having little in the way of entertainment.

March 1st. We heard this morning that poor Kettle had slipped in a frozen open drain and broken a leg on his way back to the hospital last night. His S.B.A.(D) has had to go to Murmansk for an Exit Visa. This is worrying as it will make me the senior D.O. present and I am wondering if I shall have to stay here to take his place, otherwise the hospital will be without a D.O. till the Admiralty sends out another on the next convoy. I am not keen on the idea at all! The sooner we leave the better as far as I am concerned.

In the afternoon we all went to a nearby hillside where the locals were skiing. Many of them lent us skis and we all had a go. It was quite a sight to see "Jolly Jack" careering down the hillside with his bell-bottom trousers flapping in the wind as he dodged the pine trees.

That evening I went up to the hospital to see Kettle and found him quite bright and cheerful as he will be sent home on one of our ships and so get away from this awful place.

The hospital looks to be a very hastily built rough and ready affair of bricks and mortar, much of which is suffering from the frost. The whole area is surrounded by open drains, fortunately frozen at this time of the year. The top floor housed the British, who were mostly survivors from sunken ships. There was only one wash-basin on the ward and it had only one tap which delivered cold water and the outlet led into a bucket! The Heads (toilet) was just a large sand tray in one corner and the whole place stank to high heaven.

March 2nd. Our R.A.F. passengers came back on board again to return to UK as the Russians would not give them permission to land, much to their

Figure 10

Iced up, heading North.

disgust. I reckoned they were lucky! also we have now got seven Russian Embassy staff. One Colonel, one Captain and the rest Comrades.

In the evening we had an excellent Russian Concert party on board. About thirty of them who called themselves The Choir and Concert Party of the North Russian Grand Fleet. They gave several shows through the ship and one for us in the Wardroom. They had the usual Tumblers, singers and accordionists and gave a very good show. The final item was announced as that Well Known Russian Folksong "It's a long way to Tipperary"! Afterwards we gave them supper and refreshments. One of the lady accordionists sat next to me but she had no English and everything I said to her she replied "Niet" meaning "No". Obviously she had been warned about sailors!

March 3rd. I heard that Kettle has been taken on board *Belfast* as a cot case and so will soon be back in U.K. We left Vaenga at 1100, it was still very cold 15°F. The surgery scuttle (porthole) was thick with ice with about three inches of it round the edges on the ships side. The other ships are white over so I guess we are too. There is much ice on the foc'sle and the sea has a layer of what is known as Arctic Smoke above it caused by the sea being warmer than the air. The guard rails round the deck are nine inches thick with ice from the spray freezing as it comes aboard. We closed up for the passage of Bear Island Straits from 1500 onwards, sleeping as usual on a stretcher in the bathroom flat, being brought a jug of cocoa and a Tiddey-Oggy for supper.

March 6th. We fell out at 0630 after a fairly quiet night and are now rapidly leaving the convoy behind though we heard that one ship was torpedoed during the night, most of the crew of 53 being saved. We had one dive-bombing attack during the day but there were no casualties. Now proceeding to Seydisfjord to oil.

March 8th. Having oiled we left Seydisfjord again to look for the convoy (at 1530).

March 9th. Blowing hard again and more ice on the surgery scuttle, however I managed to do a crown during the day. We chased a suspect spotted on the Radar but it turned out to be a solitary merchantman. The convoy turned up at 0445 so we left for Scapa along with *Belfast* and *Cumberland*.

March 11th. We had the usual "end of term party" in the Wardroom and I had my squeezebox out for a good sing-song which our R.A.F. people, who will be leaving us soon, thoroughly enjoyed. There were a good crowd and we have got to know them well. We arrived at Scapa at 0700 and left again at 2000hrs for the Clyde where the R.A.F. will be leaving us.

March 12th. We had a comfortable trip down for once and arrived off Greenock at 1800. I went ashore to ring my brother George who was stationed at Faslane on the Gareloch but unfortunately he had gone on leave so I had a hasty meal at the Tontine and went back to the ship.

March 13th. Warm and sunny as we left Greenoch at 1300 and sailed down the Clyde past troop ships, aircraft carriers, hospital ships and liners past Dunoon, Arran, Mull of Galloway, the Isle of Man and Northern Ireland meeting a large incoming convoy on the way escorted by one small corvette.

March 14th. I opened my scuttle at 0700 just in time to see the Longships Lighthouse which I had last seen back in 1935 from the hotel at Lands End which was also visible and which Mary and I visited while on our Honeymoon.

Later we passed the Wolf Rock Lighthouse followed by the Eddystone Lighthouse and Portland Bill Lighthouse, all clearly visible, and lastly came the Isle of Wight and Portsmouth harbour where we arrived at 1800, having had an escort of Spitfires all the way.

On arriving at Portsmouth I received a signal from the Admiralty instructing me to go on a course at the famous Maxillo-Facial hospital where the N.Z. surgeon Archibald McIndoe was doing wonders in restoring badly injured R.A.F. crew with his Plastic Surgery. I also received a signal to say that I was being relieved by a Surg. Lieut. Dennis Laverick and that I was being appointed to a shore establishment.

When Laverick arrived I took him along and introduced him to our Captain, who, after welcoming him to the ship said:

"Do you play the Squeezebox?"

On being told that he didn't the Captain said:

"Well, you have fourteen days to learn!"

March 30th. I rejoined the ship at the end of the course and was then sent on leave. On my way through London I called on my "boss" Surg. Rear-Admiral Fletcher at the Admiralty who informed me that I had been appointed to a shore establishment, namely *Cabot* in Wetherby!

POSTSCRIPT: On **Christmas Day, 1943** *Norfolk* was in action with the *Scharnhorst* which had come out from its hiding place in a Norwegian fjord to attack one of our convoys. The *Norfolk* managed to get some hits on the German ship but received two hits herself, one midships and one on "A" turret. As explained to me by the Warrant Ordnance Engineer Officer Lewis H. Molden who was at his station at the other end of the ship when the turret was hit, he found he was no longer in communication with them so went along to investigate. He found that the shell had entered the base of "A" turret, fortunately going between the hardened steel rollers on which the turret rotated or it would have exploded. It then passed through the cordite hoist, which again was luckily empty at the time, and then passed out between the rollers on the far side and exploded outside the ship. The Royal Marine Lieutenant in charge of the turret was completely unscathed though somewhat shocked and believed that they had been hit by a 4" shell! It turned out to have been an 11" armour piercing shell. One man in the turret was killed and others badly burned by the blast as the shell went through.

The other shell hit the ship midships, ploughed through the deck of the Office Flat, dived down into a workshop full of heavy machinery where men were working, and exploded nearby. Some of the machinery broke loose and that together with the explosion and fire caused a number of deaths and injuries. The blast penetrated upwards into the cabins along that side of the

Office Flat and crushed them all up into the space of about a foot! The end one had been the Chapel and the next one had been mine!

While I was at Wetherby I heard that the *Norfolk* had come up to the Tyne dockyard for repairs so I went up to see the damage, which was pretty horrific. Next morning when I went up on deck one of the messenger boys came up and said the Commander wished to see me. So I went along to find him and he said:

"No it's not you I want Toothie - it's our present Toothie!"

I thought it was rather nice that the lad should remember me when I had been out of the ship six months.

Life After *Norfolk*

Introduction

I left *Norfolk* in May 1943 and was appointed to *Cabot* - a Stoker's training establishment which had been evacuated from Bristol to Wetherby and incidentally caused much amusement to the locals because of the Naval Pinnaces just over the fence where the young matelots were taught the rudiments of rowing, - on dry land.

Here I found another ex-Leeds University dental officer, namely Frank A. Gostling who had seen service in the Merchant Navy before qualifying in 1942.

The Officer-in-Charge of *Cabot* was Capt. Fanshawe R.N. who was a real martinet and not at all popular. It took some time to convince him that I really did live near at hand and was not just "Out on the Town" whenever I slept "ashore". And when I rode in one morning on my motor-bike while he was taking Divisions he really did get annoyed. And when, shortly afterwards, on the 30th June I received my half stripe and became a Surg. Lieut. Cdr. that was about the last straw.

There was quite a lot of spare land between the various accommodation blocks in the camp, so the Powers-that-Be decided that something must be done for the Dig for Victory Campaign by having the gardeners cultivate it. Which they did, planting cabbages everywhere. Except one patch at the back of the Sick Bay overlooked by the Dental Department, being a large triangle with concrete paths round about. So the Dental Department had the idea of cultivating it themselves. Everybody joined in, officers and staff. But we planted flowers and all through the summer we had a fine show. There was a young forest of sunflowers in the centre surrounded by masses of annuals of every variety - much to the delight of the Wrens going on weekend leave who would beg "a bunch for mum".

However, the Dental Department did come up for commendation on one occasion. It happened that Frank Gostling and I were standing chatting outside the Sick Bay one day on our way to lunch in the wardroom when we heard the sound of a low-flying plane obviously in some sort of trouble as it was misfiring, popping and banging as it flew over us slowly losing height in the direction of our local small town, Wetherby. As it went out of sight I said to Frank:

"If it has any luck it will miss the town and land on the Golf Course."

Almost immediately there was a dull crump and a column of black smoke rose above the trees so we dashed to the Sick Bay phone and informed the Officer of the Watch on the Main Gate who promptly called out the Ship's fire tender, the crew of which achieved much kudos in the local paper for having got to the scene before the local Fire Brigade.

The Captain was not popular with my boss either, Surg. Cdr. Maclean R.N.V.R. He had some trouble with a leg and was waiting to go into hospital about it just after I had been into Harrogate Hospital with Sciatica in my right leg. There had been rumours for some time that the Stokers were leaving, so when Maclean was sent for to go into the Naval Hospital in Sherborne, Dorset he insisted that I must let him know the instant that the Captain departed. So the day he went, in July 1944 I sent him a telegram with a hymn number to look up. This was from Kipling's *Recessional*:

"The Captain and the Kings depart"

which caused much amusement and curiosity when Maclean requested a Hymn Book. He was the last person to have any religious inclinations.

When *Cabot* and the Stokers left, the ship became *Demetrius* and the Writers and Supply Assistants were moved up from Highgate, London. The name later being changed to *Ceres*, maybe because she was "the Goddess of Plenty."

By **Christmas 1944** the European War was coming to an end and we were just beginning to get the better of the Japs. We already had some bases in Australia so I approached my boss, Rear-Admiral Fletcher at the Admiralty with a view to getting an appointment "Down Under". I thought it might give me a chance to see the land of my Birth, New Zealand, and all my relatives there.

My first appointment, to the Dental Dept. at Warwick Farm, Sydney, *Golden Hind* was cancelled and when I later saw the place I was very glad as it was on a Race Course, some way out of Sydney and surrounded by sandy desert which was blowing all over the place.

Shortly afterwards I received another appointment with a letter from the Admiral which vaguely said that "the ship was going in the direction that I required."

The ship turned out to be the *Aorangi*, formerly of the Union Steamship Co. of New Zealand, and not to be confused with the crack Dutch Liner *Oranje* which by then was a hospital ship and which I came across later, in the Pacific, and which was staffed by N.Z. doctors and nurses.

Figure 11

Aorangi

With *Aorangi* to Manus

and Hong Kong

About the ship

In peacetime *Aorangi* had been a cruise liner on the Auckland-Sydney-Vancouver run. She belonged to the USSCo. i.e. "Union Steamship Company of New Zealand", built on the Clyde in the '20s, and was the first diesel engined passenger liner. Captain and Deck Officers were N.Z. but the crew were Sikhs, Pathans, and Goanese. She had been adapted by the Admiralty as an Accommodation ship and a 100 bed hospital installed together with a full staff of nurses, three doctors and Sick Bay attendants. The forrard hold now contained a desalination plant and another hold was the ship's cinema.

The First and Second class lounges were preserved intact, with even a grand piano. And there were First and Second class dining rooms. I had a Surgery and a separate dental lab. and a Petty Officer Dental Steward, who had been at Royal Arthur, Skegness for the whole of the war up to then. And in the lab. two young dental mechanics, barely out of their apprenticeship.

The *Aorangi*'s native crew consisted of Pathans or deck wallahs, stokers, or Og-wallahs, and Sikh engine room wallahs. Their Chief Serang was a magnificent figure named Mohammed Akbar Khan. He was said to own a couple of farms near Bombay and would-be workers had to bribe him (squeeze) for the privilege of working in his engine room. Then there were the Goanese stewards, all with very Portuguese names like Fernandez, Pereira and da Costa and they were intensely proud of them. The ship's barber was a Goanese and about the only one who could speak English. He would appear in my surgery doorway holding some unfortunate native by the ear saying "This boy Sahib, very poor boy Sahib, very sore tooth Sahib, you fix?"

The ship's crew had never had a dentist on board before so when the time came ultimately for me to leave the ship some of them came to the surgery, nearly weeping at the thoughts of losing their "nice kind tooth-doctor Sahib."

I was appointed to the ship on **March 19th 1945** and joined her on the Clyde. My younger daughter, Penelope, was born on the 26th and I just had time to dash home and see her before sailing on the 31st from the Tail o'the Bank'.

We were not a very big convoy, two light carriers, a radar ship, a dozen merchantmen and an escort of four destroyers. Once out of the shelter of the Clyde it became fairly rough so I did not spend much time on deck but turned in early and did not wake till 0700 next morning.

We spent the first week installing and fastening down our lab apparatus and finishing off the jobs that had not been done in the dockyard. Then I had to instruct the young mechanics about the use of acrylics which were fairly new at that time. The material was much better and easier to use than vulcanite and we could make teeth with it as well as dentures. Within two weeks I had made and fitted a Jacket crown.

All the naval personnel and passengers on board were dentally inspected and I was amazed to find one Royal Marine without any teeth whatsoever. He had recently had his own extracted and insisted on joining the draft so as to be with his mates, relying on obtaining dentures wherever he landed up. He was most surprised and highly delighted to be fitted out on board.

On **April 2nd**. the first casualty, due to the rolling of the ship occurred. The steriliser fell of its bracket and smashed its plastic handle so I obtained a long strip of copper from the ship's plumber (who also made a new handle for me), wrapped it right round the steriliser and screwed it to the bulkhead.

During the first week we lagged behind the convoy somewhat due to trouble with a fuel injector. (The *Aorangi* engines had been modified by the Admiralty and constantly gave trouble).

5th April. Today the ship held Emergency Drill when everybody had to turn out. Also the Oerlikons were exercised which sounded just like old times.

We have changed course and are heading Easterly, towards the Med. The two carriers and some of the merchant ships are to leave us here to go into Gibraltar while we carry straight on. Tangier with its white houses was plainly visible as were the snow-capped Atlas Mountains beyond.

8th April. "On white cap covers". It was now getting quite warm and sunbathing was becoming popular. Our route to the Far East was by Suez Canal, Bombay, Columbo, and Trincomalee. We reached Port Said and the entrance to the Suez Canal on **13th April** passing the statue of de Lesseps, the Frenchman who constructed the canal on the way in. (The statue was later destroyed by the Egyptians during the Suez war). We were not due to start through the canal till the following day so we went ashore for a look round and had a good meal at the Hotel Splendide but pestered all the time by beggars and Gully-Gully boys with their conjuring tricks, and offering leather work, postcards and out-of-date newspapers for sale. All the usual entertainments were closed on account of the death of Roosevelt.

We did not enter the canal till 1600hrs and then I spent most of the day on deck watching the busy boat traffic. Several trains passed, an army despatch rider and one man on a camel. South bound ships have to stop and tie up when they meet one north bound as they have priority, and as we met three ships on our way through we did not get clear of the canal till 0730 the next day when we stopped at Port Tewfik (Suez) to drop our Pilot also the Canal Searchlight which had been specially fitted in Port Said for the night journey. Then it was away, down the Gulf of Suez with its red sandy mountains on each side. Nothing whatever to be seen but a few dhows. It was very hot indeed and Rig of the Day became Tropical Rig and here also I saw the "Southern Cross" for the first time and lots of Flying Fish. 3,000 miles to Bombay.

17th April. Today I saw a couple of deck hands with toothache. One was called Ibraham Hassan, which sounded like a pantomime character. The lab. is very warm in the blazing sun so I got some butter muslin from the stores to put over the windows to stop the glare. (Note, that being a liner both the surgery and the lab. being on the Upper Deck had windows and not port holes). Still no black-out as this is considered a safe area.

19th April. The ship passed Perim during the night, and today Aden but there was nothing much to see. Lots of white houses and mosques but not a patch of green to be seen anywhere, even through the Bridge glasses. We now have 1,660 miles to go to Bombay. It is slightly cooler out of the Red Sea though the surgery temperature is still $84° - 86°F$! I have several showers every day and am wearing as little as possible. Today in spite of the heat I did ten fillings, four extractions, three try-ins and several other assorted jobs, including two natives with toothache.

20th April. During the day I wear a light singlet, and shorts, plus my surgery jacket, while in the evening I discard the singlet and wear the

Regulation white jacket, shorts, long white stockings and white shoes. We have a large block of ice for drinks during the day, also for keeping the wax from melting away when doing denture work.

22nd April. Iced coffee for breakfast every morning these days, together with stewed fruit. Hot dishes are out of favour though they still appear on the menu. I spent the afternoon being shown round the ship's refrigerators by the refrigerator engineer, a Scotsman. They are vast and of course, extremely cold, particularly the cold meat store at 15°F.

23rd April. Today occurred the episode of the native who wanted one tooth out. He first removed his sandals, then his red fez, sat himself in the chair and opened his mouth. I had a look inside and saw three roots of a broken down upper molar. So I said: "Three piecee tooth." He replied in no uncertain terms "No, one piecee tooth." Eventually I gave up, injected, and in due course very carefully removed all three roots, but only showed him one. Honour was satisfied. He jumped out of the chair, replaced his sandals and fez, saluted and said, "Boat Boat salaam," meaning thank-you very much! Apparently I have quite a reputation as a tooth doctor sahib already.

24th April. We arrived in sight of Bombay at 1130. Six thousand two hundred miles from home. There were lots of dhows, feluccas and other sailing craft about, also the *Mauritania*, *Strathmore* and several other troop-carrying liners that had discharged their complement of troops ashore for the long train journey across India to fight the Japs. The city appeared to stretch an immense distance around the bay and conveys an impression of pastel pinks, brown and green. I changed some money on board. One Rupee - 1/6d. but did not go ashore as a mail was expected.

25th April. Today I went ashore in the ship's cutter and landed at the Gateway to India, the steps where the Viceroys have traditionally landed and near the *Taj Mahal* Hotel. I contacted Surg. Cdr.(D) Turner, the port Dental Officer who invited me to dinner at his flat. His address was Earl's Court, The Marine Drive. Meanwhile I looked around some of the city then had lunch at the Minden Fleet Club.

Bombay has some very fine city streets and handsome buildings, but around every corner is a native quarter with shoe makers, tailors, metal workers working away on the pavement bazaar style. And that night, returning from the Turner's there were rows of people sleeping on the pavements, in doorways, and every odd corner, very often on just a bit of old carpet. Tiny children, usually unclad, sleeping beside beggars who were mostly deformed. Otherwise it was very colourful and interesting but it is quite true about the red stains of betel juice everywhere on the pavements, it looks exactly like blood.

26th April. I worked in the morning then went ashore at 1530 with some of our doctors. We took a "gharri" up to Malabar Hill where there are some fine gardens known as the Hanging Gardens because they are built over a reservoir. There was a lot of very clever topiary work with trees trimmed to look like every animal imaginable and in between were areas planted with flowering plants enclosed by box hedges being clipped and kept in shape by natives squatting on the ground.

27th April. Got ashore at 1630, after it had cooled down a bit, and took a "gharri" to the Crawford market. It is more a section of the town than a market as we know them. Every street seemed to specialise in some particular such as fruit, flowers, carved wooden boxes from Kashmir, tiny monkeys, colourful birds, and brassware. I bought myself a small teak beer mug with a silver lining which I still have also some small items of scented sandal wood. From there I met Surg. Lt. Barr, one of our doctors and our First Lieut. Sid Mitchell at the Yacht Club for a meal. The dining room was vast and palatial and you could hardly see the roof for dozens of rotating fans attempting to cool the air.

28th April. We moved out into the bay today prior to leaving tomorrow so wrote letters and posted off my purchases.

29th April. Left Bombay at 0930 bound for Columbo, 883 miles. Had a first cholera inoculation, it is said that 150 a day are dying from it in Calcutta. We had bananas or rather plantains for dessert. The first banana I have seen for a very long time.

One day, after I had got to know the Head Serang, of the Engine Room, Mohammed Akbar Khan, and treated a few of his staff, I thought I would go down below and have a look round, so I went down a long, almost vertical, polished steel ladder and at first could not recognise where I had landed. Then it dawned that I was standing on one of the cylinder heads of a bank of four, on the Starboard side of the ship, there being another similar bank on the Port side. The main deck of the engine room was a long way below me down more ladders. Here I found the Serang among his voice pipes, dials and engine room telegraphs which were his means of communication with the Bridge. From down here the engines looked enormous, like the side of a house. Each bank had four separate cylinders on a common crankcase, like the early cars and the crankcase had four doors or inspection hatches along the side so that big ends and con-rods could be examined and if necessary replaced whilst at sea. Around the sides of the engine room were hung enormous spanners and even some spare con rods, at least fifteen feet long.

There was no gearbox or gear lever for going astern. When the signal came from the bridge both watches of the engine room hands were involved and the procedure was something as follows:

1. Shut off fuel to both engines. This was done by closing valves controlled by large steel wheels three feet in diameter and each operated by two men.

2. When the engines had stopped another similar valve was opened admitting compressed air which forced the pistons back in the opposite direction.

3. When the engines were running in the astern direction the compressed air was shut off and the fuel valve opened once more when the engine would continue running. This operation had to be done for each engine and repeated when the order came for "Slow Ahead".

If a fairly sharp turn was required such as turning into a harbour only one engine went astern while the other continued as normal. It was easy to see why the air compressors, which gave much trouble were so important as the ship could not go astern without them.

1st May. Arrived at Columbo today and went ashore to see Surg. Capt. Williams who is now Fleet Dental Surgeon for all this area. I had last seen him at Scapa where he was Fleet Dental Surgeon aboard *King George V*. He remembered me from my *Norfolk* days and made me very welcome. Then I visited the local hospital with Iain Bergius, one of our doctors who hails from Glasgow, before having lunch at the Grand Orient Hotel, known as the GOH apparently. In the afternoon we toured the town in rickshaws, and admired the jewellery for which Columbo is famous but did not buy. Colombo is a big contrast after Bombay, being much smaller and very much cleaner.

2nd May. Left Columbo and went round the island to the large Naval port of Trincomalee which has an anchorage the size of Scapa only the surrounding islands are covered with jungle and thick vegetation. Trincomalee was occupied in peacetime by wealthy residents of Columbo who used it as a base for yachting and fishing. It is now the main base for the Eastern Fleet. Here I found some old friends of my *Norfolk* days including Lieut. Cdr. Langford who is now P.T. Officer here, also a fellow toothwright Peter Wilde of Doncaster who is well set up in a bungalow on the quay side with a motorbike and a yacht.

In the afternoon we went ashore and walked to a sheltered sandy beach for a bathe. The water was so warm, it must have been 80°F with shoals of colourful little fish swimming everywhere. Back on shore I tried to photograph a lizard but he was too quick for me. In the evening I had dinner with Pete Wilde in their Wardroom. He collected me and I rode pillion on his Ariel driving through country that looked very like parts of Scotland. We fed with two more Toothies, McCulloch and Turnbull, from *Wolfe*.

6th May. I had Wilde, McCulloch and "Razzle" Langford on board for lunch after which we went for a very hot walk through a jungle of coconut palms, flowering trees, with numerous tropical coloured birds flying around. There was no breeze and it was very hot and sticky. In the evening "Razzle" took me for a meal to their Officer's Club somewhere deep in the jungle, formerly known as the Welcome Inn where we heard that the European War should be over at any moment as our forces, the Americans and the Russians were closing in on Berlin.

8th May. We left Trincomalee regretfully at 0800 bound for Fremantle 3,120 miles. Today I had my second cholera jab. Later we heard that Germany had capitulated and our Captain decided to Splice the Mainbrace so we hoisted the Gin Pennant inviting our solitary escort to come aboard.

They replied:

"Much regret unable - will be with you in spirit."

So I asked my surgery lads and some friends along to my cabin for a few beers and later on the wardroom put on a very good Rum Punch.

9th May. There were some very thick heads this morning, what with the rum punch and the cholera jab and the rolling of the ship did not help matters. We were able to listen to the broadcast account of the celebrations in London and stood to attention for the King but could not hear him. We wished we were back home to join in the celebrations.

Two days later, we crossed the Line and had the usual ceremony. I took part in the procession with my Squeezebox along with King Neptune, his "wife" Aphrodite and the traditional policemen and bears. The Captain, Commander, doctors and I were all found guilty of various offences and ducked in spite of having crossed the line before but it was good fun. Most of the ship's company then had their turn and finally King Neptune and his Court were all pushed into the pool.

11th May. We had our first rain today since leaving Gibraltar.

14th May. It has got much cooler as we approach Australia. It is windy with white tops on the waves. It seems to be a normal state of affairs in these parts that as the sun sets and the temperature falls the clouds drop their load

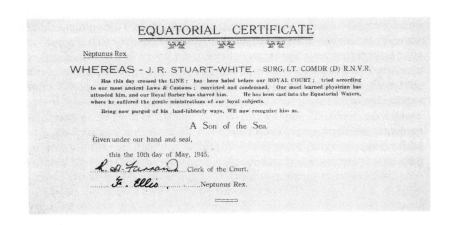

EQUATORIAL CERTIFICATE

Neptunus Rex

WHEREAS - J. R. STUART-WHITE. SURG. LT. COMDR (D) R.N.V.R.

Has this day crossed the LINE ; has been haled before our ROYAL COURT ; tried according to our most ancient Laws & Customs ; convicted and condemned. Our most learned physician has attended him, and our Royal Barber has shaved him. He has been cast into the Equatorial Waters, where he suffered the gentle ministrations of our loyal subjects.

Being now purged of his land-lubberly ways, WE now recognize him as,

A Son of the Sea.

Given under our hand and seal,

this the 10th day of May, 1945.

.... Clerk of the Court.

.... Neptunus Rex.

Figure 12

Proof from King Neptune Himself!

of rain and we get a downpour. Today we officially changed from "Whites" back to "Blues".

18th May. Today arrived in sight of Fremantle. There was an awful flap on board when we received a signal saying that we should have gone to Darwin! But later it transpired that it was intended for our escort frigate *Odzano*. We berthed at 1500hrs.

19th May. I had a walk into Fremantle and my diary says it was a bit of an anticlimax at first sight as with its corrugated iron roofs and the large corrugated iron water butt outside every house it looked like a Gold Rush town. However, there were some good shops and a Woolworths, and the people were exceptionally hospitable.

In the evening I went into Perth by train, one shilling and six pence return First Class. The railway follows the Swan river closely being built up most of the way with quite neat looking bungalows and the train stopped at each of the twelve stations on the way.

I had a meal at the Officer's Club, a half-chicken and *et ceteras* for three shillings and six pence then had a walk round admiring the shops and neon lights before catching the train back.

21st May. I had Simpson who is Dental Officer of *Adamant*, a submarine depôt ship, over for lunch. There is some confusion as to our role here as we were expecting to be an Accommodation Ship for the Submariners who are based here but they all appear to have found accommodation ashore so we shall probably be sent round to Sydney.

22nd May. I spent the day ashore with our P.M.O. visiting the Naval Hospital at Hollywood, Fremantle where I met an Australian army Dental Officer who invited me to their Dental Association meeting next week. Also visited *Leeuwin*, their Naval Base and met a Royal Australian Navy Surg. Lieut. Cdr. (D) Amos, from Melbourne. The P.M.O. and I then had dinner in town and returned to the ship by train.

23rd May. The local Missions to Seamen organised a dance for the ship's company where we were introduced to some of the local people and there were many invitations to their homes.

24th May. A lot of people have joined the ship here so I took the opportunity of examining them and found quite a lot to do. Many of them are taking passage with us back to their homes in Sydney.

26th May. Major Roy Kent and Major Glaskin of the Australian Dental Corps were aboard to look around the ship and were very impressed by my department. In the evening we went to a ship's dance at *Leeuwin*. Our Captain and Commander also attended. I found a W.R.A.N. (Women's Royal Australian Navy) there who was born in Knaresborough, Yorks. but had come out with her family as a youngster.

30th May. I was taken into town by the manager of a Freezing Works, where sheep go in one end and come out the other as frozen mutton after which I was taken to the Swan Brewery for a Chemical Society lecture on Penicillin and later, of course, toured the brewery.

1st June. Taken for a drive around the town by one of the Shell Company's engineers. We went via the University of Perth and through King's Park. The University is built in the Italian style and is a very handsome building and the surrounding park overlooks the Swan River.

This was followed by a visit to a Cocktail party organised by Western Australian Broadcast Co. who gave us tickets to a number of events and were very good to us.

2nd June. Today was the first day of winter in this part of the world. At home we would have called it a nice hot summer's day.

6th June. This evening I was taken to the first Symphony Concert of the Season, held in Winthrop Hall, of the University. I was introduced to the Conductor, Sir Ernest MacMillan and to the Solo Pianist, Betty Munro George who played a Liszt Concerto, Mendlesohn's Fingal's Cave and some Delius. I was given a good seat, in the front row of the Gallery and felt quite important!

7th June. Today I was taken by my Refrigeration Engineer friend for a drive into the surrounding country, first to Guildford where the first settlers put up their homes then to a little vineyard called Houghton started by the Ferguson family a hundred years ago. Here we sampled a number of wines and brought a good selection away with us.

8th June. Friday. Troops started to come on board this morning - all good things have to come to an end sometime. The old *Aorangi* has made a good impression on a lot of people both in Fremantle and Perth and everybody is sad to see us go - except those whose homes are in Sydney and want to be on their way. I rang all my new friends to thank them for their hospitality also ABC - Australian Broadcasting Co. who had done so much for us.

We have twenty extra officers in the lounge and one lady who is the wife of a Colonel in the Sick Bay.

10th June. We rounded Leuuwin Cape during the night (South-western extremity of Australia) and began the journey across the Great Australian Bight passing the tree-lined cliffs of Albany on the way.

11th June. Next day the weather started to blow up. It was much cooler with quite a heavy cold looking sea. We hear that a cyclone is approaching the South-east coast and that two small coasting vessels have already been blown ashore and wrecked.

12th June. The weather has improved but we have been very lucky as the Australian Bight can be very rough indeed.

13th June. We have now crossed the dreaded Bight and rounded Wilson's Promontory which is the southernmost tip of Australia and nearest to Tasmania. It is very rocky with small isolated inlets dotted about. The area is known as the Bass Straits and can be very dangerous in bad weather. We have turned the corner and are proceeding North-east. There was nothing to see on the Point but a lighthouse and signal station and a few stumpy trees. It is misty, dull and a bit chilly.

14th June. We moved up the coast today but could not see much because of mist and rain squalls. Soon after dark the lights of Sydney showed as a dull glow over the horizon. Botany Bay, just South of Sydney was easily recognised by its lights through the entrance, and soon Sydney showed up as the ship approached the Heads, which are the big cliffs on either side of the harbour entrance. We lay in the outer harbour all night surrounded by shipping including many aircraft carriers.

In the evening we had a party for all the Aussie passengers who are leaving us here which did not finish till 0300.

15th June. I, in common with many others felt very poor this morning as when the bar closed last night the Aussies produced all the drink they had brought on board, thinking we were a Trooper and therefore dry and I think the "gin" must have been methyl alcohol. Towards midday we moved up under "Our Bridge" into the upper harbour to our berth at No:5 Darling Harbour and it really did look as though our tall masts would never go under the bridge. Once alongside the ship's own gangway with her name on it was brought out and folk could get on and off.

In the evening I went for a short walk into the town and brought back a dozen bananas and a custard apple. The latter has a green knobbly skin and the inside has a custardy consistency and tastes like melon.

16th June. The next few days were spent cleaning up the surgery after our long passage and visiting the Naval Stores in Glebe for necessary replacements. After reporting to the Fleet Dental Surgeon a visit was made to Warwick Farm (*Golden Hind*) Surg, Cdr. (D) Daniels R.N. and to the Royal Auxiliary Hospital, Surg, Lt. Cdr. (D) Horne R.N. who in turn visited the ship. I had last met him in Rosyth and though I did not know it then I was to finish my Far Eastern War at this hospital.

23rd June. Today we had the Fleet Dental Surgeon, Surg. Cdr. Sam Ross Wallis R.N. on board to inspect the surgery and laboratory. He made various suggestions towards helping us combat the heat and arranged for us to receive more suitable fans. Each week the Fleet Dental Surgeon circulates a list of ships in harbour together with ships they have to contact if needing dental treatment.

29th June. Doc. Bergius and I were given a weeks leave. We took the train up through the Blue Mountains to Katoomba which is the centre of a popular Health Resort area and here we stayed for a few days exploring the area which has historic connections. It was many years before the early settlers found their way through the much forested mountainous region that makes up this area and ultimately discovered the flat plains that lie beyond. From Katoomba we took the train again to Bathurst a small country town beyond the mountains and thence to Goulburn by a local bus, stopping on the way at Trunkey Creek, a former Bush Ranger's haunt to eventually catch the Melbourne Sydney Express at Goulburn and so back to Sydney on July 2nd.

4th July. Our P.M.O. has been sent to a hospital at Port Stephen, a little further up the coast as he is having chest trouble. A new P.M.O. has arrived and seems quite a nice chap. He is a Surg. Lieut. Cdr. R.N.

Back in Glasgow we had been supplied with electric heating appliances for the lab which were unsatisfactory so when I reported this to the Fleet Dental Surgeon he arranged for me to have gas burners and supplies of bottled gas. This duly arrived whilst in Sydney and our plumber fitted it all up and welded up a "fiddle" on the lab. bench to stop boilers etc. from sliding about.

6th July. I heard that we are leaving Sydney tomorrow so went ashore to report to the Fleet Dental Surgeon who announced that he would be visiting us later.

Figure 13

Western Route of the *Aorangi*

7th July. We left Sydney at 1100 today, turning North after passing through Sydney Heads. The voyage down the harbour is very interesting and colourful with ships coming and going, ferries darting from one side to the other, hundreds of yachts and beautiful houses and gardens lining both shores.

10th July. It has got noticeably warmer and we have changed into whites. I started to examine 120 new ship's company, who are mostly "Boiler Cleaners" from *Tyne*. Fortunately there is not a lot to do for them.

11th July. Today we passed our first coral islands, one of which was complete with a tank landing craft piled up on it. We are passing up inside the Great Barrier Reef which extends right up to the north of Queensland, the islands are low and mostly wooded surrounded by reefs and sandy beaches. Much warmer 82°F and rain from time to time.

12th July. We spent today passing New Guinea. It is extremely mountainous and appears to be completely covered with jungle.

13th July. We arrived at Manus, a large volcanic island in the Admiralty Group just 3° below the equator and belonging to Australia. We berthed at 1600 in a large bay enclosed by a coral reef and there are numerous other islands about, most of which seem to be covered with coconut palms. The island looks quite mountainous at one end and densely wooded. The Americans have been here for some time and have a large base with hospital and church and have made roads across the island from coral.

14th July. *Montclare* has arrived so I went over to see Surg. Lt. Staple R.N. who is now Senior Dental Officer here. I found him sitting up in his bunk wearing a sarong and suffering from shingles.

We discussed the allocation of ships for treatment, and as we are now a member of Admiral Bruce Fraser's Fleet Train, which is poised for the recapture of the Pacific there are many ships and much work for the few dental officers present at the moment.

16th July. There is plenty of work already, today I have seen officers and men of the *Flamborough Head* and the oilers *Serbol* and *Rapidol*.

17th July. I also have some patients from the Australian Navy, e.g. H.M.A.S. *Cessnock, Bendigo* and *Launceston*.

On Manus we had an interesting life among the Yanks on the surrounding coral islands. One called Pitiloo had a football pitch, also a wonderful lagoon which was enclosed by two coral reefs and so was shark proof. It was only about six feet deep all over and contained a wealth of tropical fish of all shapes, sizes and colours. I made myself a pair of underwater glasses out of dental plastic! which

ure 14

Eastern Route of the *Aorangi*

83

although not completely water-tight served their purpose and others were keen to borrow them.

Life continued in this fashion, working in the cool of the morning and occasionally evenings, except when there was an emergency. Most days we would go to the lagoon to cool off and then perhaps visit some of the Americans we had got to know.

While at Manus the Indian crew celebrated Ramadan when they are not allowed to eat during the day. The exception being Coconut! so they went ashore and climbing the coconut palms like monkeys hurled them down to those below.

The Yanks had built a large open air church - the "Chapel of the Islands" - where some of the services were conducted in Pidgin English for the benefit of the natives. There was also a large open-air cinema. As you went in there was a table on which were two basins, one of salt tablets and one of mepacrin (against malaria).

Fortunately, as we were anchored off we were out of reach of mosquitoes so did not have to take the mepacrin which made people yellow. Land crabs used to swarm over the tracks at night looking like mobile Cats Eyes in the Jeep's headlights.

28th July. Today the Fleet Dental Surgeon Surg. Cdr. (D) Sam Ross Wallis flew up from Sydney. He was accommodated on board for several days during which I accompanied him as we went round the Fleet visiting the various dental officers and making enquiries into their working conditions. The F.D.S. is good company, very efficient and does all he can for his dental officers. We also went ashore on Manus where there is no one at the moment, but a D.O. is expected.

30th July. The F.D.S. gave a one man show to the troops on board and one Aussie was heard to say:

"Why can't our people send us comics like him!"

1st August. Today the F.D.S. went over to Ponam a small island with an airstrip further along the coast, to see D.O. Basil Pett.

2nd August. I went ashore to see the F.D.S. off. He is flying back to Sydney. Lieut. Martin, the new Base D.O. for Manus arrived to take over his appointment ashore.

During this period (July - December 1945) the character of the ship changed from time to time. Originally designed to accommodate spare submarine crews she had sailed from Sydney with 120 ratings who consisted of Boat Pool operators, boiler cleaners and Fleet train Porters. These used to go out of the ship during the day to their various jobs returning on board for their evening meal.

In Manus the 8th Australian Mine Sweeper Flotilla had been allocated to this ship and proved to be very "tooth-conscious" and although they had been unable to obtain treatment for some time they showed evidence of careful work in the past and were very grateful for treatment received on board *Aorangi*.

In common with most small ships they were liable to sail at very short notice and often the signal telling us so would arrive after they had left in which case we operated on our own ship's company.

At Manus, distances between ships were relatively great and often a dental party would have to leave their ship at 0800 in order to arrive in *Aorangi* for 0900 and if, as sometimes happened the boat broke down or the weather became bad the party was apt to be missing for some time. In fact a signal was once received from the Captain of a ship at 1630 "Request whereabouts of my dental party sent to you at 0800." As they had not arrived it was impossible to help.

When patients went on draft before their dentures were finished the dentures were sent with them to be completed on arrival back in UK.

6th August. The first news came through about "The Bomb" on Hiroshima in Japan. We do not know what it is but from all accounts it is pretty devastating.

Three days later, **9th August**. another Bomb was dropped on Nagasaki. They are apparently Atomic Bombs and are very secret. The Japs offered to surrender but refused to do so unconditionally so the Powers that be told them it must be unconditional or else. See Appendix.

15th August. The Japanese have now surrendered unconditionally. I had been for a bathe and got back just in time for Splicing the Mainbrace. After dinner all the ship's sirens started blowing, and there was quite a display of rockets, and Very Lights. There was a large bonfire ashore which turned out to be a store hut that the Yanks had set on fire and they were dancing round, throwing their hats in the air and shooting them full of holes. We were not allowed ashore so had to content ourselves by watching the fireworks and sounding off the ships sirens.

Although the war was supposed to be over we were still blacked-out at night because of the possibility of there being Japanese subs about who had not heard the news. Life continued in much the same way for the next fortnight and our department was kept very busy by all the Australian and British minesweepers and other small ships that were in the harbour.

Sunday 26th August. The ship's Chief Electrician Mr. Munro had a bad accident today. A boat lowering winch that he was testing jammed and he was endeavouring to free it, when suddenly the heavy iron handle swung round and hit him on the forehead fracturing the frontal bone. He was rushed off to a neighbouring hospital ship, the *Vasna* and most amazingly was still conscious.

27th August. I went over to *Vasna* to see Mr. Munro, he looks pretty bad and the surgeon says he has only a 50/50 chance.

Later I had dinner with their D.O., Surg. Lieut. Simons, and looked round the ship which is quite small and only carries six Sisters.

28th August. I spent most of the day ashore. I found a small Native Museum containing curios, model outrigger canoes, shells, butterflies and a collection of Japanese exhibits.

29th August. There was no shore leave as we are hoisting boats, ready for departure tomorrow.

I heard that today Mr. Munro had died. Not very surprising really as he looked terrible when I saw him on Monday. Very sad.

30th August. Several Aussies and Americans came aboard for a final drink and to say Goodbye to us. I also received a signal from Lieut. Betts of the U.S. Navy wishing us *Bon Voyage*.

We sailed 1400 with *Montclare*, *Resource* a light carrier and a few mineseweepers. We passed round the North side of Manus and saw other islands of the Admiralty Group in the distance. Some of the smaller ones look just like a row of coconut palms on the horizon.

31st August. The ship is still blacked out for our voyage North, no smoking is allowed on the upper deck and no private wireless sets may be used. All of which can give one away to an enemy submarine. We did think we had finished with black-out but the Commander says there are still enemy subs about.

There was another unfortunate occurrence today. Our new Doctor was found in his bunk this morning unconscious and it turned out later that he had taken an overdose of drugs and was dead. There was a Court of Enquiry on board attended by Officers and doctors from the *Pioneer*. It was a very unhappy affair as he was well liked. A quiet chap who did not talk much about himself, very artistic, musical, also painted and sketched and did seem a bit highly strung, but a good shipmate and joined in all our activities.

He was buried at sea, just over the Line at 1500.

1st September. We returned one of the doctors to *Pioneer*, keeping the other to assist Doc. Bergius.

2nd September. It was my Dental Steward Gordon Connolly's birthday today and we had a party for him in the Assistant Cook's cabin. Connolly is a good chap and has settled down well to life on board. Unfortunately he suffers badly from Prickly Heat which makes life very uncomfortable for him in the Tropics and he cannot wait to get into cooler climes.

One of the main engine compressors went west this morning and we slowed down in consequence and got left considerably behind the others. It is a very breezy day with spray blowing on board and agreeably cooler.

4th September. Passed a few islands today and met a few merchant ships returning from up north. No sooner had the compressor been put right when the second one broke down. Towards midnight we approached a narrow passage between islands west of the Philippines. They were close enough to see in the dark and our convoy went into single line ahead. Quite warm on deck.

6th September. Sailed right in among the Philippines today passing Mindanao, Bataan, Corregidor and Manila, though as the latter lies at the far side of a large bay there was nothing to see except one or two mosque-like buildings and a forest of masts. The islands are hilly and rough and covered with coconut palms and other vegetation. They are bright green, looking rather like Lakeland Fells - except the green is a forest of trees.. jungle.

Arrival at Hong Kong.

9th September. Sunday. I was up at 0700 today to see the approach to Hong Kong. It first appeared as an island off a rocky shore with mist rolling down from distant mountain peaks as the sun warmed them up. It was a fantastic coast, just like the illustrations in a child's fairy tale. At first there was no opening visible till we rounded another island and saw the first ship of the convoy enter a narrow passage between high cliffs, each adorned with gun battery sites, fortunately no longer occupied. Soon our turn came and we made our way through between sampans and junks fishing in the entrance, to anchor within sight of the town, with Victoria, the capital of Hong Kong Island on the one hand and Kowloon, on the mainland, on the other.

There is no shore leave as things are far from settled ashore as yet and one still hears sporadic gunfire due, it is said, to bandits rather than armed forces. We are surrounded by dozens of small sampans, mostly manned by women and children. Some are attempting to barter while others are content to smile and wait for things to be thrown to them. They do not hesitate to fish bread out of the water and dry it in the sun. Some are clean and tidy, others scruffy and dirty but all look very happy and pleased with life and above all glad to see the British Fleet back and the departure of the Japs.

On arrival in Hong Kong the ship's character changed once again and became an accommodation ship for officers and men whose duties were ashore, e.g. Salvage, Radio, Dockyard and Forward Drafting Pool. There were Armed Guards, and Anti- Piracy Patrols going out every day aboard river steamers. But accommodation was gradually provided ashore and on 25th October the Rear Admiral Fleet Train moved in with his staff. At the end of which time the ship reverted to accommodation for officers and men awaiting passage home for release.

10th September. Monday. It is still very hot, and I wish I had some film as it is quite the most picturesque anchorage that we have had. We are surrounded by tall crags of a reddish colour with grass covering most of them right up to the very tops. In the distance is *Tai Mo Shan* behind Kowloon, which is the highest mountain around here and it too appears to be grass covered to the top.

The buildings ashore look quite sound but I am told that most of them are just hollow shells due to looting.

11th September. At least two bodies have come floating past on the tide. Meanwhile there is plenty of barter going on but the Chinese appear to have peculiar ideas of values - it seems to be roughly one pound equals one American dollar, equals two bars of soap, equals one packet of cigarettes.

The Dental Officer of the carrier *Vengeance* was on board today and brought me some denture work. He has been ashore and says shops have plenty in them - at a price. Tonight Doc. Bergius and I are to visit *Pioneer* for dinner.

Soon the hospital on board was busy looking after and rehabilitating POWs from ashore and later from the JAP prison camps up North before sending them on to Australia. Most of them were not much better than living skeletons.

12th September. Managed to get ashore today with Iain Bergius and McKinnis who is D.O. of *Pioneer*. Our objective was to investigate the condition of the R.N. Hospital. We found it after a walk of twenty-five minutes through a poorer part of town. It had been very neglected and much wilful damage done. One operating table was out in the drive while furniture, papers, books, drugs, bottles were lying everywhere in endless confusion and an all pervading odour of Japs. The hospital had been used partly as barracks and partly as sick-bay and there were blood stained dressings lying all over the place. (Also an SS Jaguar in fair condition). We had a short walk back through the town. Most of the buildings looked sound but were boarded up. The population are thin but do not look like famine children. They seem to live on a diet of dried fish, rice, dried seaweed and vegetables.

13th September. I borrowed a ship's boat this morning and delivered some denture work to *Vengeance*, also visited Staple, on *Montclare* and described to him the conditions ashore. We are to go again tomorrow. The hospital ship *Gerusalemme* has arrived today from Manus.

Round the harbour side in Kowloon were a number of "go-downs" or warehouses four or five stories high and there the Jap prisoners were exercised. Each one had to carry a large sack of flour on his back, run up the steps to the top of the building, along and down the other end - *ad infinitum* suitably encouraged by our troops till they were dropping with fatigue.

14th September. It poured solidly all day so did not go ashore. McKinnes from *Pioneer* came aboard in the evening. He said they had pinched the S.S. we found at the hospital for their commodore. Only needs a new tube and a battery.

15th September. Today I went over to *Montclare* for lunch with Staple and then went to the R.N. Hospital again to do an inventory. It was decided that the hospital was in such a ruinous condition that it was unusable and that the other hospitals in the town should be investigated. It rained again but luckily we got a lift back to the dockyard, where I had a chat with Doc. Partington who helped us out for a while in *Aorangi*. He is in sole charge of the dockyard sickbay and has his hands full.

The Fleet Dental Surgeon has announced that A.J. Staple, the Surg. Lieut Cdr. R.N. from *Montclare* is to be Senior Dental Surgeon in Hong Kong and that I rank second to him in seniority, which gives me a bit of kudos.

The sampans surrounding the ship acted like a taxi rank and were used by anyone wanting to go ashore. Once when I was in one, crewed by the usual old woman, young girl and small boy, the small boy managed to fall overboard. Nobody bothered, they made no effort to go about or drop the sail. Fortunately I was sitting in the stern and just managed to grab him by the collar and yank him aboard and the old lady was profuse in her thanks. I was told later that its all a matter of Fate. If he had managed to swim and save himself - O.K., but if he had drowned then that was Fate and couldn't be helped.

17th September. Today I went over by sampan to Kowloon and was taken for a run around by Norman Hineshaw R.A.F. in his Sunbeam Talbot.

We went to the outskirts of Kowloon and saw the road zig-zagging over the mountains to Chinese territory which is out of bounds. Kowloon is said to be a cheaper place to live than Hong Kong but it is extremely crowded. Three Q.A. Sisters and three V.A.D.'s joined the ship today to help in our hospital. They have already been for a week in Stanley prisoner of war camp over on the other side of the island.

20th September. Peter Young, D.O. of *Resource* came over for lunch. He used to be at *Cabot*, Wetherby and was relieved by Frank Gostling so we had a good yarn about old times.

22nd September. I went into town with Doc. Bergius and two of our Sisters. We wandered around through the narrow streets, all swarming with vendors selling every conceivable article, mostly junk. Did not buy anything but have my eye on a camphor- wood chest and will take one home if possible. Again it was very hot and steamy so we found a little cafe and had Chinese tea. It tasted something like an infusion of straw but was thirst quenching. The little waitress kept on filling up the tea pot with hot water but it still came out a pale straw colour. An unlimited quantity for four people worked out at one dollar H.K. = 1/3d. In the evening Bergius and I went over to *Resource* and were shown round their workshops - vast, and very like those of *Hecla*.

23rd September. Doc. Iain Bergius' cousin, Adam Bergius turned up from Manus. He is in submarines, and we have *Sidon*, *Scotsman*, and *Spearhead* tied up alongside and they use our accommodation.

I am now in the usual routine whilst in harbour, i.e. Priority for treatment to crews of other ships which is keeping me very busy.

28th September. Went over to *Vengeance* this evening for dinner with Lillicrap for whom I have done quite a lot of denture work. I endeavour to get all work sent to me processed and back to their ship within three days.

29th September. Very hot indeed today so did not go ashore after work. In the evening Bergius and I went over to *Ballarat* a Royal Australian Navy Corvette. They were entertaining some Aussie ex-POWs and I took my squeezebox along and gave them a sing-song which they seemed to enjoy. *Ballarat* brought us back about 0300 after a very pleasant evening.

30th September. Sunday. I did a little shopping and bought four yards of cream silk at eight dollars HK a yard i.e. about ten shillings. Then I went for a look round the fish market where all the fish are swimming around in shallow tanks and you chose which you want. There were small turtles, squid, eels, lobsters, crab, etc.

Behind the city of Victoria, which is the capital of Hong Kong the land rises up to a steep hill known as The Peak, which seemed to be covered with beautiful looking houses and in peacetime the wealthier you were the higher up The Peak you lived as the air was fresher. But on closer examination all the beautiful houses were mere shells. Every item of furniture was missing and so was all the woodwork. No wood floors, window frames or doors. All removed by the Chinese for firewood. Fridges, cookers and so on, which were too heavy to move were abandoned where they had been dropped, by the wayside.

In Kowloon the lads found a dance hall where they had what were known as taxi dancers - you bought a few tickets and then sought out a likely looking partner, presented your ticket, had your dance and then sat down again and so on. One night I required the loo and found it was upstairs. I looked around as I reached the top and there on the far wall was a row of six toilets, each with its door wide open and each with a girl sitting in it and all yattering away at the top of their voices. On seeing me all the doors slammed shut simultaneously with a bang.

Another time I was in a drinking place of some sort and needed the loo. I made my way through the throng and found two doors. I made for the one which I thought had the "Men" symbol on it. As I approached the door opened and a girl came out. She didn't turn a hair as we met in the doorway.

In the restaurants, each individual party had its own partitioned off area. You could hear your neighbours but couldn't see them. One night the Doc. and I visited a small one in Kowloon. We were ushered in and a couple of girls came to help us choose from the menu. You were provided with a bowl of sunflower seeds as a starter and the girls demonstrated how to split them with your teeth, extract the kernel and then spit out the husk. When the meal arrived an old man and a tiny girl came in. He was carrying what looked like a home-made one-string fiddle on which he started to make caterwauling sounds while the little girl wailed in company. The trouble was we couldn't stop them till we got the idea of paying them off.

Walking back through the streets at night there was an incessant rattling sound coming through the open windows of the apartments - everyone was playing *Mah-Jong*, rattling their pieces on the table.

The famous tramway that ran up The Peak had been sabotaged by the Japs, as had the power station, so when the submarine Depôt ship *Maidstone* arrived she tied up at the quay. Her crew repaired the power station in due course but in the meanwhile the ship produced enough electricity to run the Peak Tramway.

KOWLOON means nine dragons. The dragons being the range of mountains behind the town and separating the area from China proper. The highest was *Tai Mo Shan*. It had a road up to the top and on it was a Jap Radar post. Some of us went up one day in a borrowed Jeep. We found the post all right but all the equipment had gone apart from a telephone and a map of the surroundings on the table. There was an excellent view over the islands and surrounding paddy-fields.

On the way out of town we had passed a constant procession of Chinese coolies each carrying a bamboo over the shoulder with a jerrycan on each end. This contained "nightsoil" collected from all the flats and houses in the area and was being taken out to the paddyfields and vegetable plots where it was used as fertiliser for their vegetables for which the Chinese are famous.

On board *Aorangi* I was kept busy as I not only had our own crew including Goanese, Sikhs etc., to look after but all the small ships of the fleet, who of course did not have Dental officers. On top of that there were by now D.O.s ashore and they had no lab facilities and they helped to keep us busy. One time this brought me some sort of notoriety as one of the young D.O.s ashore had been asked to repair a denture for a Japanese Admiral POW and having no lab. sent me an apologetic letter asking if I could help. Naturally I said yes. But next week in the local "China Mail" was an irate letter from a matelot who complained bitterly about a Jap POW getting treatment free when presumably he would have to pay. Which was rubbish. Fortunately the local C.O. vindicated me. I don't know what happened to the Jap but at least he would be able to eat his last meal.

On the **1st. Oct.** a colleague from *Cabot*, Wetherby, Surg. Lieut. Frank Gostling R.N.V.R. turned up on *Aorangi*. He was contemporary with Pete Wilde of Trincomalee while at the Leeds University Dental School.

It turned out that Frank had been appointed to MONAB VIII, (Mobile Naval Air Base) and had come out with them in the Carrier "Striker". He had been supplied with a caravan equipped as a dental surgery but unfortunately the caravan together with all his equipment was buried at the bottom of the ship's hold where it had been severely damaged on the voyage.

However, he had managed to get accommodation on the first floor of a good-looking semi. Number 190, Prince Edward Road, Kowloon, in a better part of the city and near the airport. The ground floor was occupied by the Naval Sick Bay so he was in good company. He had been given a dental chair and managed to borrow the necessary equipment and was soon in business. And on **11th October** he was back on board for lunch with four repairs for my lab. to do.

For the remainder of the month I was kept busy with R.N. and R.A.N. Merchantmen, and emergency work for the native crew, while the hospital was busy rehabilitating POWs and members of the forces prior to sending them on to Australia to complete their recovery before sending them home. At this time I was seeing twelve to fourteen patients a day, most of whom were from other ships.

On **5th December** my Petty Officer Sick Berth Attendant Gordon Connolly got a draft chit home and his relief, S.B.A. Sharp joined the ship and took over his duties. P.O. Connolly had been a very efficient Dental steward and in spite of having no previous experience at sea very quickly settled down into the routine. (See Appendix re him qualifying post war as L.D.S.)

12th December. Gordon Connolly left the ship for onward passage home and demob in UK.

Christmas 1945 in Hong Kong was a wild and noisy affair. Long strings of fireworks were suspended from roof tops. Lit at the bottom they cracked and banged all the way up to the top to dispel the devils. During the festivities some of us were invited into the homes of Chinese businessmen we had got to know and were initiated into the art of an authentic Chinese meal. Quite an experience.

Meanwhile, back on **1st November 1945** the office of the British Pacific Fleet had appointed Surg. Lieut. (D) Swain R.N.V.R. to *Aorangi* to replace me, while on **3rd November** Surg. Lieut. Cdr. Watson was appointed in a signal from the Medical Director, Admiralty whereupon the appointment of Swain to *Aorangi* was cancelled. On **10th December** a signal was made to Admiralty enquiring as to the whereabouts of Surg. Lieut. Comdr. Watson, followed by another from Commodore Hong Kong on **29th December** which brought the reply from C-in-C East Indies that Watson was no longer available and that Surg. Lieut. (D) Reid R.N.V.R. was on passage in *Jamaica* and expected to arrive in Singapore on **2nd January** for onward routing to join *Aorangi*. Finally, on **10th January** a signal was received from C-in-C British Pacific Fleet appointing Surg. Lieut. Comdr. (D) J.R.S. White R.N.V.R. *Aorangi* to H.M.H.S. *Vasna* Vice Surg. Lieut. (D) Simons.

On **14th January 1946**, after several false alarms my relief turned up and I left for Sydney in the little Indian hospital ship, *Vasna*. In Sydney, the R.N. Hospital at Herne Bay was without a dental officer so the Surg. Capt. grabbed me and I was in business once more. And after working there for a while I put in for leave in New Zealand which I managed to get after some argument and so my original ambition was satisfied. I crossed to New

Zealand in a small coaster, the *Karatu* also belonging to the U.S.S. Co. of New Zealand, of which my uncle, C.G. White was a Director. We only had ten passengers, most of whom were returned POW 's from Japan and a few Servicemen returning home. The ship was "dry" but fortunately we had been warned and took measures accordingly. A fast ship takes three days to cross from Sydney to New Zealand, a normal passenger ship takes five but we took eight. It was very hot and we spent most of the time playing cards on deck or watching the antics of the porpoises around the bow.

Once in New Zealand, where I was met by relatives everywhere, the dockyard obligingly went on strike and no ships could leave so I was able to continue my leave staying with relations from one end of the country to the other until at last I was found a berth in the passenger ship *Tamaroa* where I shared a cabin with a retired sea-captain who was looking up old friends in ports all over the world.

One day I got into conversation with an elderly Chinese and asked where he was making for.

He replied, "Hong Kong"

So I asked, "Which part."

And he said, "Number 190, Prince Edward Road, Kowloon!"

So I was able to reassure him that his home, unlike most of the others in the area, had not been vandalised and was in good condition due to the fact that Japanese Officers had occupied it all through the war. And that my friends who were occupying it at the moment would soon be leaving. The old chap was quite overcome and much relieved at the good news.

After a few more weeks at the Sydney Royal Naval Hospital I finally came home in the aircraft carrier *Indefatigable* with the rest of the hospital, and a cabin full of goodies for the folk back home.

And that was my Far East War, which made up for all the horrors of the Russian Convoys.

J. R. Stuart White, *B.Ch.D.*
Surg. Lieut. Cdr. R.N.V.R.

Appendix

1. Originally, in order to "save face" they wished to retain their Emperor as Sovereign Ruler. However, America, Britain, Russia and China agreed that "unconditional" meant just that - unconditional, and the statement from Washington read:

```
From the moment of surrender the authority of the Emperor
and the Japanese Government to rule the State shall be
subject to the Supreme Commander of the Allied Powers.
   The Emperor will be required to authorise the signature
by the Government of Japan of the surrender terms and the
acceptance of the Potsdam Agreement, to issue commands to
all forces under their command to cease operation, to
surrender their arms and immediately transport prisoners of
war to places of safety where they can quickly be placed
aboard allied transports.
   The ultimate form of government of Japan shall be in
accordance with the Potsdam Agreement and be established by
the freely expressed wish of the people. The armed forces
will remain in Japan until the purposes set forth in the
Potsdam Agreement are achieved.
                    signed: James E. Byrne,
                    Secretary of State,
                    Washington.
```

2. **Captain John S. Litchfield OBE,** 1903-93. Captain Litchfield had a long and successful career in the Royal Navy and was appointed to *Norfolk* as Commander and Executive Officer in 1941 and later as Acting Captain when the ship's Captain became ill. In later years he became Captain of *Vanguard.*

3. **Surgeon Comdr. (D) Samuel Ross Wallis R.N.** unfortunately barely outlived the end of the war in the Pacific. He collapsed and died in Sydney whilst taking part in his favourite recreation, namely as Rugby Football Referee.

4. **Sick Berth Attendant E.G. Connolly,** who had been an office clerk pre-war became so interested in Dentistry that on de-mob he enrolled as a

dental student at the University of Liverpool and qualified as a dental surgeon in 1953.

Of this I knew nothing until I met him at the Blackpool Annual General Meeting of the British Dental Association. He had set up practice in Nottingham and I met him later on numerous occasions.

5. **Surg. Lieut. (D) F. A. Gostling** on de-mob went into the Schools Dental Service in Leeds after which he went into private practice.

6. The **Reverend A. Kenneth Mathews, OBE**, DSC. 1906-93 was the *Norfolk's* well-loved Padré. Having taken a liking for the sea he spent his early days in tankers, joining the R.N.V.R. in 1939. He spent the rest of the war in *Norfolk* where he took his turn in the Air Defence Position and during action he would move around the ship giving encouragement or administering morphine as necessary. Captain Bellars used to say that it was Padré Ken's influence that made the *Norfolk* such a happy ship.

7. In 1959 my son, **David**, having qualified as a dental surgeon at the University of Leeds Dental School, elected to follow in his father's footsteps by doing his National Service in the Royal Navy. Having completed which he elected to stay on until taking early retirement in 1990. During his time in the navy he served in *Belfast, Bulwark* and *Bermuda*, actually being aboard each one when it "paid-off" - (De-commissioned).

He also served in a number of Shore Establishments such as *Ganges, Mercury, Dolphin*, Faslane, the Royal Marine Reserve Depôt, Exton, and *Collingwood* (Portsmouth) and abroad in Gibraltar and Singapore.

8. **George Stuart White**.

After his injury during their evacuation of Cherbourg, two weeks after Dunkirk, my brother George was hospitalised for some time, and on his recovery he obtained a Commission in the Royal Pioneer Corps and was stationed in and around London for the duration of the war.

9. **J. Stuart White** (Senior).

After the First World War my father went back to Nobel's Explosive Company and his job as West Riding Agent and Explosives Expert so when the Second World War started he naturally joined the Home Guard as their adviser on explosives and Inspector of the magazines where they were kept.

Already a District Commissioner of the South-East Leeds Boy Scouts he also took on South Leeds Division on account of the shortage of man power. Not content with these activities he worked two allotments providing welcome food for family and friends. He finally lived to the ripe old age of ninety-two.

INDEX

INDEX